Best of the Historic West

Best of the Historic West

For information, contact:

StarsEnd Creations, Inc.
8547 East Arapahoe Road, #J224
Greenwood Village, Colorado 80112

PRINTING HISTORY
First Edition
First Printing August 2000
ISBN 1-889120-14-6

Library of Congress Control Number 00-091843

Published by
Pantry Press
8547 East Arapahoe Road, #J224
Greenwood Village, Colorado 80112

Printed and bound in the United States of America
10 9 8 7 6 5 4 3 2 1

TABLE OF CONTENTS

INTRODUCTION

The term 'Old West' invokes any number of images, depending upon the cultural background of the listener. For the most part this image is one of myth and legend; a time and place peopled with figures that were larger than life and who performed monumental deeds in a raw land. Part of this legend is that of the cuisine enjoyed by the people on the frontier. Being isolated from their eastern cousins these hardy people developed their own brand of cooking, based upon the time-honored recipes they brought along on their westward migration.

This tradition continues today, as exemplified by the recipes developed and used by the members of the Colorado Dude and Guest Ranch Associaiton, Distinctive Inns of Colorado and the fine historic hotels who participated in this project. Without their kind cooperation and enthusiastic support we could not have completed this cookbook. To them we give a hearty thanks.

In the process of developing this cookbook it was decided early on to present the reader with a view of the cuisine from the West that might prove to be surprising. This was done by combining the best recipes in use at the elite guest ranches, bed & breakfast inns and hotels from around the Colorado and Wyoming region. The result is quite a varied mix of styles and cuisine which we hope you will find of interest.

On the pages to follow you will find every type of cooking style represented. Be it simple and easy to use dishes that busy people can prepare at a moment's notice, to more elegant recipes for that special dinner, we believe you will find it in this book. It is our sincere wish that you enjoy yourself on this culinary trip to the Historic West.

Baked Goods

Applesauce Spice Bread

Preheat the oven to 350 degrees. Grease 3 mini-loaf pans. In a mixing bowl, combine the flour, baking soda, baking powder, cinnamon, allspice, nutmeg and salt; set aside. In a separate bowl, combine the sugar, applesauce, oil, milk and eggs; beat well. Stir the dry ingredients into the liquid, combining well with as few strokes as possible. Stir in ¾ cup walnuts.

Pour the batter into the prepared pans. Combine the brown sugar and ⅓ cup walnuts and sprinkle over the top of the batter. Bake for 40 to 45 minutes. Cool for 10 minutes before removing from the pans.

"What a delightful place to stay on my birthday! They've thought of everything—every convenience to make the weary traveler feel comfortable and at home. In terms of the B & B's I've stayed in across this country, this is a 5-star operation!"

Judy

Temperature: 350 degrees
Cooking time: 1 hour
Yields: 3 mini-loaves
Can be stored for 1 to 3 days.

2 cups all purpose flour
½ teaspoon baking soda
½ teaspoon baking powder
½ teaspoon cinnamon
½ teaspoon allspice
¼ teaspoon nutmeg
½ teaspoon salt
1 cup sugar
1 cup applesauce
2 tablespoons milk
⅓ cup oil
2 eggs
¾ cup walnuts, chopped
¼ cup brown sugar
⅓ cup walnuts, chopped

Buttermilk Banana Bread

Temperature: 350 degrees
Cooking time: 50 to 60
 minutes
Yields: 1 loaf

1 cup sugar
½ cup oil
2 eggs
1 cup (2 medium)
 bananas
½ cup buttermilk or
 sour cream
1 teaspoon vanilla
1 ½ cups flour
1 teaspoon baking soda
½ teaspoon salt
½ cup or more walnuts
 or pecans (optional)

Preheat the oven to 350 degrees. Grease a 9 x 5-inch loaf pan. Beat together the sugar, oil and eggs. Add the bananas, buttermilk and vanilla. Add the flour, baking soda and salt; mix well. Add the nuts and pour into the prepared pan. Bake until done or a toothpick inserted in the center comes out clean. Allow to cool for 5 minutes, and then remove from the pan. Finish cooling on a baking rack.

This Banana Bread is a bit more unique than a traditional recipe, because it is made with buttermilk or sour cream.

Cinnamon Raisin Bread with Maple Glaze

In the bowl of an automatic mixer, combine the warm water, maple syrup and yeast. Set aside for 5 to 10 minutes to activate. Meanwhile, heat oatmeal and add the butter, mix to combine. When yeast is ready, add 3 cups of the flour and mix briefly. Add the oatmeal, salt, raisins and cinnamon. Do not add the salt directly to yeast; it will kill the yeast instantly. Add the remaining flour in half cup increments until dough comes together and is slightly tacky to the touch. Turn dough out into a greased bowl, cover with plastic wrap and place in a warm spot until doubled in size.

Spray a 9 x 5-inch loaf pan with non-stick spray. Turn dough out onto a lightly floured work surface. Gently knead the dough into a rectangle and roll into a loaf, pinching the seam. Place dough into a loaf pan seam side down. Place in a warm area to proof. Let the dough rise to the top of the loaf pan and place it into a preheated 350 degree oven. Bake for approximately 30 to 40 minutes. The crust should be a deep golden brown.

Remove from pan and place on a cooling rack. Once the bread is cool, heat the glazing syrup until warm. Whisk in the powdered sugar. Adjust consistency with warm water until a heavy cream consistency is reached. Pour the glaze over the top letting it run down the sides.

Temperature: 350 degrees
Cooking time: 30 to 40
  minutes
Yields: 1 loaf

  1 cup warm water (110
   to 120 degrees)
  $\frac{1}{4}$ cup maple syrup
  $\frac{1}{2}$ tablespoon active
   dry yeast
  5 cups (more or less) all
   purpose flour
  1 $\frac{1}{2}$ cups oatmeal, hot
  1 $\frac{1}{2}$ tablespoons butter
  1 teaspoon salt
  $\frac{2}{3}$ cup raisins
  2 teaspoons cinnamon

Glaze-
  1 cup powdered sugar
  3 tablespoons maple
   syrup

Grilled Rosemary Flatbread

Temperature: grill
Cooking time: 10 minutes

6 cups water
2 ½ tablespoons active
dry yeast
1 ½ tablespoons salt
20 cups all purpose flour
(approximately)
4 sprigs fresh rosemary,
roughly chopped

Measure out the 6 cups water; temperature should be about bath temperature to the wrist. Add the water to a large mixing bowl. Add yeast and let rest 5 minutes. Meanwhile, chop the rosemary and set aside.

When the yeast mixture is good and frothy add some of the flour. Add the salt and rosemary, and continue adding flour until it reaches bread dough consistency. Turn out to a large bowl and cover. Place in a warm area until dough has doubled in size. Punch down and let proof again. Scale to desired size, brush with olive oil and grill on a hot grill. Cook about 5 minutes on each side. Remove, cut and serve warm with olive oil and/or balsamic vinegar.

"I really enjoyed the food. It was great."

Kera
Pearland, TX

Lemon Loaf

Cream butter and sugar together in a large bowl. Beat in eggs, one at a time. Sift flour, baking powder and salt into a small bowl. Carefully stir lemon rind into flour mixture. Add flour mixture and milk to creamed mixture alternately, beginning and ending with the flour mixture.

Pour into greased loaf pans. Bake for 45 to 55 minutes or until done. Use a toothpick to poke holes in the tops of the hot loaves. Mix the Lemon Sauce ingredients together, stirring until dissolved. Pour Lemon Sauce over bread. Cool 10 minutes in pans and then turn out onto rack to cool completely.

Needs no accompaniment, but for the lemon lover, serve with lemon curd.

"One of my common complaints to major hotels is that it is very difficult to receive a pot of coffee or tea in my room at night without paying an arm and a leg...but at the Briar Rose, having a cup of tea ANYTIME is NO PROBLEM!"

John and Marti

Temperature: 350 degrees
Cooking time: 45 to 60 minutes
Yields: 4 small loaves
Can be stored for a month or so frozen

2 sticks (8 ounces) butter, softened
2 cups sugar
4 eggs
3 cups all-purpose flour
2 teaspoons baking powder
½ teaspoon salt
2 tablespoons grated lemon rind
1 cup milk
¼ teaspoon vanilla

Lemon Sauce-
⅔ cup sugar
½ cup fresh lemon juice

Lightner Creek Cornbread

Temperature: 425 degrees
Cooking time: 20 to 25
  minutes
Yields: 8 servings
Can be stored frozen

1 ½ cups flour
5 teaspoons baking
  powder
4 tablespoons sugar
1 ½ teaspoons salt
2 ½ cups coarse ground
  corn meal
2 eggs, beaten
6 tablespoons butter,
  melted or drippings
2 cups milk
Green or red roasted
  bell peppers, onions,
  olives or chives up to
  ½ cup

Combine all the dry ingredients and mix thoroughly. In a separate bowl combine all the wet ingredients and mix thoroughly. Add the dry and wet mixtures together, careful not to over mix. Pour into a lightly oiled 9 x 9-inch pan. Bake until firm to the touch and browned. It can be made in a larger dish to cook more quickly. This can be made days before and it freezes well too.

Mexican Cornbread

Combine oil, eggs, buttermilk and corn. Combine cornmeal, flour, baking powder, salt, baking soda, cayenne pepper, cheese, green pepper, onion and jalapeno. Mix well, stir in buttermilk mixture. Pour into a buttered and floured 13 x 9 x 2-inch pan or a hot 10-inch cast iron skillet.

Bake at 375 degrees for 45 minutes or until a toothpick inserted into the center comes out clean.

You may sift all dry ingredients together and store in a zip lock bag and whisk all the wet ingredients together and store in a separate zip lock bag. Place both bags on a flat cookie sheet in the freezer to store overnight. These can be used for overnight cookouts or camping trips. When ready to use, stir contents of the zip lock bags together and bake in a cast iron Dutch oven. There are no high altitude adjustments needed.

"Just wanted to thank you again for my wonderful vacation at Sky Corral. You and your staff have a very special way of making guests feel welcome and comfortable."

Chris

Temperature: 375 degrees
Cooking time: 45 minutes
Yields: 12 servings

- **½ cup cooking oil**
- **2 eggs, beaten**
- **1 cup buttermilk**
- **1 cup (8-ounce can) cream-style corn**
- **1 ¼ cups cornmeal**
- **¼ cup all-purpose flour**
- **2 teaspoons baking powder**
- **1 teaspoon salt**
- **1 teaspoon baking soda**
- **¼ teaspoon cayenne pepper**
- **½ cup (4 ounces) sharp Cheddar cheese, grated**
- **½ cup green pepper, finely chopped (optional)**
- **1 medium onion, finely chopped**
- **1 jalapeno pepper, finely chopped and seeded**

Parmesan Pull Aparts

Temperature: 425 degrees
Cooking time: 15 to 45
   minutes

Frozen bread dough of
   your choice (allow to
   thaw overnight in
   refrigerator)
4 to 5 tablespoons
   Parmesan cheese,
   grated
3 to 4 tablespoons
   parsley flakes, Italian
   Seasoning, or Oregano
1 teaspoon celery seed
1 teaspoon garlic
   powder
1 teaspoon onion flakes
3 to 4 tablespoons
   sesame seeds
1 stick margarine,
   melted and cooled
   slightly

Generously grease a small loaf or round bak-ing pan with butter; set aside. In a small bowl, combine all the dry ingredients. Chop the bread dough into smaller, bite-size pieces. Dip the bread in the melted butter and roll in the dry ingredients. Drop in the pan, allowing pieces to pile up in a random fashion, but still covering the pan fairly evenly. Bake in a 425 degree oven for 15 to 45 minutes, depending on bread baking directions.

Garnish with fresh parsley. Serve by turning pan upside down onto a serving plate (one for each table). Allow your guests to pull and eat! Good served with any Italian-style meal such as spaghetti or lasagne.

This is also wonderful as a breakfast bread. Use a combination of cinnamon, nutmeg, gin-ger, allspice, pumpkin pie spice, etc. along with brown sugar, raisins, chopped nuts, dried chopped fruit, etc. with the melted butter and bread dough. Wonderful!

Poppy Seed Bread

Preheat oven to 350 degrees. Grease and flour the loaf pans. Mix the eggs, milk, oil and sugar together in a mixing bowl. Add the flour, salt and baking powder. Blend with a mixer until smooth. Pour the mixture into the prepared loaf pans. Add the poppy seeds and vanilla, mixing until well blended. Bake for 1 hour or until a cake tester comes out clean.

Temperature: 350 degrees
Cooking time: 1 hour
Yields: 2 loaves

3 eggs
1 $\frac{1}{2}$ cups milk
1 $\frac{1}{8}$ cups oil
2 $\frac{1}{4}$ cups sugar
3 cups flour
1 $\frac{1}{2}$ teaspoons salt
1 $\frac{1}{2}$ teaspoons baking
   powder
1 $\frac{1}{2}$ tablespoons poppy
   seeds
1 $\frac{1}{2}$ teaspoons vanilla

Pumpkin Bread

Temperature: 350 degrees
Cooking time: 1 hour
Yields: 2 to 3 loaves
Can be stored overnight
  in the refrigerator

1 teaspoon nutmeg
1 teaspoon cinnamon
2 ¾ cups sugar
1 cup of cooking oil
4 eggs
½ teaspoon salt
⅓ cup canned pumpkin
⅔ cup water
2 teaspoons baking soda
3 cups flour
1 teaspoon vanilla

Preheat the oven to 350 degrees. In a large bowl, beat the nutmeg, cinnamon, sugar, oil, eggs and salt together. Add and mix in order, the pumpkin, water, vanilla, baking soda and flour. Grease the loaf pans well. Pour the mixture into the loaf pans and bake for 1 hour or until a cake tester comes out clean. Enjoy!

Rosa's French Bread

Combine 3 cups flour with the yeast. Heat 2 $\frac{1}{2}$ cups water to 115 to 120 degrees. Add sugar, salt and oil to the water. Add the wet ingredients to the flour mixture. Beat on low for 1 minute with a large mixer. Beat on high for 3 minutes. Stir in enough of the remaining flour to make a soft dough.

Switch to a bread hook or knead by hand for 10 to 12 minutes until smooth and elastic. Use as little flour as possible, while keeping the dough from sticking to your hands. Over-flouring can cause the bread to become tough.

Place the dough into a greased bowl. Turn over to grease the top. Cover with a towel and let rise approximately 1 to 1 $\frac{1}{2}$ hours, until dough doubles in bulk. Punch down the dough after it rises and form into French bread loaves. Place into a baking pan that has been greased and lightly coated with the cornmeal and let rise in a warm (80 degree) place again until doubled in bulk. Brush with beaten egg white and water. Sprinkle with sesame seeds or poppy seeds.

Bake at 375 degrees for 20 minutes or until golden.

Temperature: 375 degrees
Cooking time: 20 minutes
Yields: 2 to 4 loaves
The dough can also be stored in a freezer for baking at a later date.

7 to 7 $\frac{1}{2}$ cups all-purpose flour
2 packages yeast
1 tablespoon sugar
1 tablespoon salt
1 tablespoon olive oil
A small amount of cornmeal
1 egg white with 1 tablespoon water mixed in
2 $\frac{1}{2}$ cups water (115 to 120 degrees)

Angel Biscuits

Temperature: 400 degrees
Cooking time: 12 to 15
  minutes
Yields: 18 biscuits
Can be stored for 3 to 4
  days in a cooler before
  or after baking

1 package dry yeast
¼ cup warm water (80
  degrees)
2 ½ cups flour
½ teaspoon baking soda
1 teaspoon baking
  powder
1 teaspoon salt
⅛ cup sugar
½ cup shortening
1 cup buttermilk

Dissolve the yeast in the warm water and set aside. Mix the dry ingredients in the order given, then cut in the shortening. Stir in the buttermilk and the yeast mixture, blending well. Knead the dough until it's the desired consistency. You can refrigerate the dough at this point, pulling off what you want to use at later times.

Roll the dough out on a floured board. Cut the dough with a biscuit cutter and place on a greased cookie sheet about ½ inch apart. You can either let the dough rise for approximately 30 minutes or bake immediately in an oven preheated to 400 degrees for 12 to 15 minutes.

This is always a popular item at our cowboy suppers.

Light and Lively Lemony Orange Muffins

Cream the sugar, shortening, eggs and lemon juice together. Sift together the flour, baking powder, salt and nutmeg. Add to the creamed mixture alternately with the milk, beating well after each addition. Fill each cup of a greased or paper lined muffin pan ⅔ full of the batter. Bake at 350 degrees for 20 to 25 minutes. Brush muffins with the orange glaze, while still warm. Serve warm with chilled orange butter.

Temperature: 350 degrees
Cooking time: 25 minutes
Yields: 24 muffins

- 1 cup sugar
- ⅔ cup shortening
- 2 eggs
- 2 tablespoons freshly squeezed lemon juice
- 3 cups sifted all purpose flour
- 3 teaspoons baking powder
- ½ teaspoon salt
- 1 teaspoon ground nutmeg
- 1 cup milk

Orange Glaze-
- 1 ½ cups powdered sugar
- 4 tablespoons freshly squeezed orange juice
- 2 tablespoons grated orange rind

Orange Butter-
- 3 tablespoons powdered sugar
- 2 tablespoons grated orange rind
- ½ cup unsalted butter, softened

Peaches and Cream Muffins

Temperature: 350 degrees
Cooking time: 20 to 35 minutes
Yields: 15 to 20 servings

Batter-
3 eggs
2 cups sugar
¾ cup oil
2 cups milk
½ teaspoon salt
2 teaspoons baking powder
4 cups flour
2 cups peaches, diced and drained

Filling-
1 cup cream cheese, softened
⅓ teaspoon almond extract
2 tablespoons peach juice
¾ cup sugar

Topping-
⅓ cup cinnamon/sugar mixture

Mix the eggs, sugar, oil, milk, salt, baking powder and flour together in a bowl. Beat 2 minutes and stir in the peaches.

Preheat the oven to 350 degrees. Mix together all the filling ingredients, until smooth. Drop 1 tablespoon of filling in the middle of each muffin. Sprinkle the muffin tops with cinnamon and sugar mixture. Bake for 20 to 25 minutes.

For variety, this also makes a great coffeecake. After pouring the filling over the batter, take a knife and draw through the filling, making swirls. Add the topping and bake at 350 degrees for 35 minutes.

You can also mix the remaining peach juice drained off the peaches with ⅓ cup brown sugar to be used as an optional topping.

Sopapillas

Mix the ingredients for 5 minutes on medium speed with a mixer. Roll out the dough to $\frac{1}{4}$-inch thickness. Cut into squares and deep fry. Flip once in oil.

Serve with powdered sugar and honey.

Temperature: deep fried
Cooking time: 7 minutes
Yields: 8 servings

1 tablespoon yeast
$\frac{1}{8}$ cup warm water
4 tablespoons sugar
$\frac{3}{4}$ cup milk
$\frac{1}{2}$ teaspoon salt
1 egg
3 $\frac{1}{2}$ cups high gluten flour
1 tablespoon oil

Supreme Potato Rolls

Temperature: 400 degrees
Cooking time: 10 to 12
  minutes
Yields: 3 dozen

1 cup milk
½ cup water
1 package dry yeast
1 cup cooked, mashed
  potatoes
2 eggs
⅔ cup vegetable
  shortening, melted
½ cup sugar
2 teaspoons salt
6 to 6 ½ cups
  all-purpose flour

Combine milk and water in a heavy saucepan, cook over medium heat, stirring constantly until very hot (do not boil). Cool to lukewarm (105 to 115 degrees). Stir in yeast; let stand for 5 minutes.

Combine potatoes, eggs, shortening, sugar and salt in a large bowl; mix at medium speed with an electric mixer until smooth. Add yeast mixture. Gradually add 2 cups flour, beating until smooth. Beating well, add enough of the remaining flour to form a stiff dough.

Turn dough out onto a lightly floured surface, and knead until smooth and elastic (about 10 minutes). Place in a well-greased bowl, turning to grease the top. Cover and let rise in a warm place (85 degrees), free from drafts, for 1 hour or until dough has doubled in bulk.

Punch dough down. Roll into ½-inch thickness on a lightly floured surface. Cut out circles with a 2 ½-inch biscuit cutter. Place dough circles on a greased baking sheet, ½ inch apart. You may fold the rolls in half if desired. Cover and let rise again, for 30 minutes or until the dough has doubled in bulk.

Bake at 400 degrees for 10 to 12 minutes or until golden. Brush the tops with melted butter if desired. The dough can also be stored in the refrigerator overnight or frozen and baked later.

Sweet Potato or Pumpkin Biscuits

In a bowl, mix the flour, sugar, baking powder and salt together. Cut the margarine into the dry ingredient mixture. Add the potatoes or pumpkin and the milk. Stir into a ball and roll out onto a floured surface and cut with a biscuit cutter.

Bake on a cookie sheet at 425 degrees for 10 to 15 minutes.

Temperature: 425 degrees
Cooking time: 10 to 15 minutes
Yields: 2 dozen

4 cups flour
½ cup brown sugar
1 tablespoon baking powder
1 teaspoon salt
10 tablespoons margarine
1 cup mashed sweet potatoes or pumpkin
¾ cup milk

"I can't think of a word to describe how outstanding, how superb every part of the food was! It was a delight to be served by your staff, and I do mean served, and it was an honor to eat!"

Asparagus Breakfast Torte

Temperature: 375 degrees
Cooking time: 30 to 40
minutes
Yields: 6 to 8 servings

1 package puff pastry
dough
1 pound asparagus,
blanched
½ pound ham, chopped
½ pound cheese
(Cheddar/Monterey
Jack/Swiss or combina-
tion), grated
8 eggs

Let the puff pastry dough thaw at room temperature for about 20 minutes. Preheat oven to 375 degrees. Roll out dough according to package directions. Cut circle of puff pastry to fit bottom of 9-inch Springform pan. Cut strips of dough and line sides of pan, pinching bottom edge to seal. Reserve scraps for lattice top.

Scramble 4 eggs together; cook in a non-stick skillet like a frittata. Place in bottom of pastry-lined pan. Top with asparagus spears, chopped ham and cheese. Repeat.

Piece together scraps of puff pastry. Cut strips and make a lattice crust on top. Bake in 375 degree oven until brown (about 30 to 40 minutes).

"It was a great experience to stay here, everything was great. The rooms are neat and comfortable and the food excellent. Muchas gracias."

Roberto

Baklava

Preheat the oven to 375 degrees. Melt the syrup ingredients in a saucepan. Place the filling ingredients in a food processor and process until finely ground. Layer the phyllo sheets 10 at a time, brushing between each sheet with butter. After the tenth layer, place $\frac{1}{4}$ of the filling mixture onto the phyllo. Repeat until you run out of phyllo and filling. Cut into diagonals. Bake for 30 minutes. Reduce heat to 350 degrees and bake another 30 minutes. When you pull the pan out of the oven, pour cooled syrup over hot baklava. Let cool.

Temperature: 375 degrees
Cooking time: 1 hour
Yields: 24 servings

Syrup-
  $\frac{1}{2}$ cup water
  1 slice lemon
  1 cup sugar
  1 tablespoon cinnamon

Filling-
  2 cups walnuts
  2 cups almonds
  $\frac{1}{4}$ cup sugar
  1 teaspoon cinnamon

Pastry-
  1 pound phyllo dough
  1 pound butter, melted

Breakfast Strudel with Blood Orange Hollandaise

Temperature: 400 degrees
Cooking time: 15 to 20
minutes
Yields: 10 servings

2 sheets frozen puff
pastry
17 eggs
½ cup Half & Half™
Salt and pepper
1 tablespoon butter
12 ounces assorted wild
mushrooms, sliced
6 ounces fresh spinach
½ cup Monterrey Jack
cheese, shredded
½ cup Cheddar cheese,
shredded
¼ cup mozzarella
cheese

Preheat oven to 400. Lay one sheet of frozen puff pastry on a cookie sheet to thaw. Place other sheet of puff pastry on a sheet of wax paper to thaw. Mix 15 eggs in a large mixing bowl; add Half & Half™. Whip until well mixed. Add salt and pepper to taste. Melt butter in large non-stick sauté pan. Add egg mixture and scramble until eggs are set. Spoon eggs onto thawed puff pastry leaving 1 to 2 inches around edge to seal. Layer the mushrooms, spinach and cheeses onto the eggs. Mix 2 eggs and 1 tablespoon of water in a small bowl to make a wash. Brush edges of bottom sheet of puff pastry with wash. Place the second sheet of puff pastry on top of the filling and seal around the edges. Brush top sheet with wash. Use a small knife to cut air holes into the top of the pastry. Place on middle rack in oven; bake until golden, 15 to 20 minutes. Slice immediately and serve with Blood Orange Hollandaise.

Blood Orange Hollandaise

Mix egg yolks, vinegar, juice, and water in top of a double boiler. Place over simmering water and whip until mixture begins to thicken. It is done when it runs in slow ribbons off the whisk. Be careful not to scramble the eggs. Remove from the double boiler and add butter in small amounts stirring continuously to emulsify.

Temperature: boiling
Cooking time: 10 minutes
Yields: 10 servings

3 egg yolks
1 tablespoon white wine
  vinegar
Juice of 2 blood oranges
1 pound butter, melted
  and clarified
$\frac{1}{2}$ cup water
Salt and pepper

Caramelized Onion, Tomato and Goat Cheese Tarts

Temperature: 400 degrees
Cooking time: 7 to 10 minutes
Yields: 4 servings

Dough-
  2 cups all purpose flour
  ¾ teaspoon salt
  ¾ teaspoon sugar
  6 ounces butter, cubed, cold
  5 tablespoons ice water

4 ounces Goat cheese
Roasted Tomatoes, see Oven Roasted Tomato Relish recipe
Caramelized Onions, see recipe
1 egg, beaten

Combine the flour, sugar, salt and butter in a food processor and pulse to break up the butter. The consistency should be that of coarse cornmeal. Transfer to a large mixing bowl and gradually add the ice water until the dough holds together. Keep the dough lumpy—this will make a flaky crust. Refrigerate for 15 minutes to relax before rolling out.

Divide the dough into 4 equal pieces and roll into balls. On a lightly floured surface, flatten the dough and roll to a little thinner than 1/4 inch. Place about 3 tablespoons of the onions in the center. Top with some of the roasted tomatoes and some crumbled goat cheese.

Fold in the edges of the tart, overlapping slightly. Brush with an egg wash (one egg beaten) and bake in a 400 degree oven for 7 to 10 minutes or until golden brown.

"Superb staff, fabulous food. A perfect paradise."

George & Cynthia
San Antonio, TX

Cocoa-Mocha Cream Puffs

Boil the water and butter in a pan. Add the flour to the mixture. Remove from heat and blend, until it reaches the consistency of mashed potatoes. Place in a mixer and add the eggs one at a time, beating until smooth. Pour the mixture into a pastry bag and squeeze out small ball forms onto a greased cookie sheet. Bake at 400 degrees for 30 minutes or until golden brown.

Whip the cream, adding the powdered sugar, cocoa and instant coffee. Beat until stiff and place in a pastry bag with a small tip. Squeeze the cream into the side of each puff, until it starts to over flow. Sprinkle the tops of the puffs lightly with powdered sugar.

Temperature: 400 degrees
Cooking time: 30 minutes
Yields: 30 cream puffs

Pastry-
  1 cup water
  $\frac{1}{2}$ cup butter or
    margarine
  1 cup flour
  4 eggs

Cream Filling-
  1 cup whipping cream
  $\frac{1}{4}$ cup powdered sugar
  1 teaspoon cocoa
    powder
  1 teaspoon powdered
    instant coffee

Croissants a la Orange

Temperature: 350 degrees
Cooking time: 20 to 25
minutes
Yields: 6 servings

6 large croissants, cut
into top and bottom
halves
18 ounces orange (or
apricot) marmalade
⅓ cup orange juice
5 large eggs
1 cup heavy cream
1 teaspoon almond
extract (increase by
25% for more egg cus-
tard sauce)
1 teaspoon grated
orange rind (optional)
3 orange slices for
garnish
6 strawberries for
garnish

Grease 6 oven proof bowls big enough to hold 1 croissant each (6-inch diameter). Place the bottom of the croissant in each bowl. Thin the marmalade with the orange juice and spoon 2 to 3 tablespoons over each croissant. Replace the croissant tops. Beat together the eggs, cream and almond extract, adding the orange rind if desired. Pour about 3 tablespoons of the mixture over each croissant. Spoon 1 to 2 tablespoons of the marmalade mixture over each of the croissants.

Cover and let soak overnight. Bake in preheated 350 degree oven for 20 to 25 minutes or until the mixture is set. Serve the croissants hot, allowing them a few minutes to settle. Garnish with the orange slices and a tablespoon of whipped cream, then top with the strawberries.

Dame Margaret's Lemon Bars

Cut the butter into the flour and add the sugar. Press the dough into the bottom of a 9 x 12-inch pan. Bake for 20 minutes at 350 degrees.

Juice the lemons. Add the flour, sugar, baking powder and eggs. Whip together and pour over the baked crust. Return to the oven and bake an additional 35 minutes at 350 degrees. Cool and cut into bars. Dust with powdered sugar.

Temperature: 350 degrees
Cooking time: 55 minutes
Yields: 24 to 30 bars

Crust-
  2 cups flour
  1 cup butter, softened
  1/2 cup powdered sugar

Filling-
  2 lemons
  2 tablespoons flour
  2 cups sugar
  1 teaspoon baking
    powder
  4 eggs

"Our week-long stay at Castle Marne has truly been a wonderful experience. The breakfasts and teas were delicious, the conservatory very comfortable and the entire staff very gracious. Thank you to everyone."

Clara and Garth
South Burlington, VT

Deep in Blueberry/Apple Heaven

Temperature: 350 degrees
Cooking time: 70 minutes
Yields: 12 to 16 servings
Can be frozen for 1 to 2
weeks

Dough-
  ½ cup butter, softened
  ⅓ cup sugar
  1 egg
  1 ⅓ cups flour
  1 teaspoon baking
  powder

Fruit Mixture-
  2 cups blueberries
  3 apples
  1 teaspoon cream of
  tartar
  ⅓ cup flour

Filling-
  ½ cup butter, softened
  ⅔ cup sugar
  2 eggs
  2 tablespoons flour
  1 teaspoon baking
  powder
  1 teaspoon almond
  extract
  1 ½ cups hazelnuts,
  chopped

To make the dough, beat the butter and sugar together with an electric mixer until light and fluffy. Add the egg and beat well. Mix together the flour and baking powder. Then mix all together until smooth dough is formed. Press dough in the bottom and 1 inch up the sides of a greased 9-inch springform pan.

Start the fruit mixture by rinsing the blueberries; drain. Core, peel and thinly slice the apples. Mix the blueberries, apples, cream of tartar and flour. Place the mixture on top of the dough.

For the filling, cream the butter and sugar with a mixer until light and fluffy. Add eggs one at a time beating well after each addition. Add flour and baking powder and mix well. Stir in almond extract and hazelnuts. Spoon the filling over the fruit mix. Bake in a preheated 350 degree oven for 70 minutes. Cover with foil after 50 minutes. Sprinkle with confectioners sugar to complete an outrageous brunch/lunch sweet.

"We enjoyed our stay with you. Our room was beautiful and comfortable the food superb, the staff friendly & helpful. But words fail to really describe what a lovely experience it is to stay at the Abriendo Inn."

John & Lois
Helena, MT

John's Famous Monster Cinnamon Rolls

Heat 1 cup of milk, until it registers 110 degrees on a candy thermometer. Set it aside to cool. In a small bowl or measuring cup, stir warm water, yeast, 1 teaspoon of sugar and the ginger together. Let it set, until mixture foams. In a mixing bowl, use an electric mixer to mix the butter, sugar, salt, egg and dried milk. Add the cooled milk; add the yeast mixture and mix. Change to a dough hook and add the flour to the mixture, 1 cup at a time, mixing after each addition. Turn out the mixture onto a floured cloth and knead, until smooth. Place the dough in a well-greased bowl and cover with plastic wrap. Set in a warm spot (85+ degrees), until dough has doubled in bulk. Place it on a floured board and knead out the air bubbles.

Roll the dough into a 9 x 18-inch rectangle. Spread the softened butter over the dough. In a small bowl, mix the brown sugar and cinnamon. Spread evenly over the dough. Roll the dough from the long end. Cut into 1 1/4-inch slices. Place in a heavily greased 9 x 13-inch pan. Let the dough double in bulk once again (about 1 hour). Set the oven to 350 degrees and bake the rolls for 20 to 30 minutes or until they are golden brown. Remove from the oven and let cool 10 minutes before frosting.

For the frosting, mis the butter and cream cheese with the powdered sugar and milk. Drizzle over the rolls.

Cooking time: 20 to 30 minutes
Yields: 6 servings

Dough-
   1/3 cup butter
   1/3 cup sugar
   1 teaspoon salt
   1 egg
   1/2 cup dried milk
   1/3 cup warm water
   1 teaspoon sugar
   1 package Bakers Rapid Rise Yeast
   1 pinch ground ginger
   1 cup milk
   4 cups flour
   1/2 stick butter, softened
   1/2 cup brown sugar
   3 teaspoons ground cinnamon

Frosting-
   1 package cream cheese, softened
   1/2 stick butter, softened
   1 cup powdered sugar
   1/4 cup milk

Miner's Pies
(Cornish Pasties)

Temperature: 350 degrees
Cooking time: 45 to 60
  minutes
Yields: 8 servings

3 cups cooked lean beef,
  cubed
3 cups boiled potatoes,
  cubed
¼ cup chopped onion
¾ teaspoon celery salt
1 ½ cups beef gravy

Never Fail Pie Dough-
  3 cups flour
  1 teaspoon salt
  1 ¼ cups shortening
  1 egg
  1 teaspoon vinegar
  5 tablespoons ice water

Prepare the dough first, making a double recipe. In a bowl, mix the flour and salt. Cut in the shortening, until the dough is crumbly. Lightly beat the egg, vinegar and water. Add all at once to the flour mixture. Mix just until moist.

Cook the beef and potatoes well in advance of making this recipe. In a large bowl, mix the beef, potatoes, onion, salt and gravy.

For each pie, take a small handful of the pie dough and form it into a thick circle about the size of a large dessert plate. Moisten the edge of the dough with water. Place about ¾ cup of the filling in the center of the pie dough. Fold the dough over and press down to form a half circle shape. Press the dough around the edges to seal the pie. Trim off any excess dough.

Preheat the oven to 350 degrees. Place the pies on an ungreased baking sheet. Brush the tops with a glaze made by mixing 1 egg to ⅓ cup milk. Bake for 45 to 60 minutes until light brown. Serve with more gravy if desired.

Cornish pasties were a typical lunch for miners. Their lunch pails had a lower compartment that would hold coffee, while the upper compartment usually contained a pastie. The whole lunch pail could be placed over a small fire, so that the coffee would be hot and the pastie warmed.

Pastelitos
(Little Pies)

Mix the flour, baking powder and salt. Cut in the shortening until it is well blended. Add milk and knead until it forms a soft dough. Pinch off the dough to make 24 balls. Roll 12 pieces of dough so that each piece is about 4 inches across (a little larger than fist size).

Beat the eggs, milk and salt, and cook to make scrambled eggs. Crumble, fry and drain the chorizo sausage. Mix the scrambled eggs, fried chorizo sausage, chopped green onion, green peppers, red peppers and cilantro. Evenly divide the cooked egg mixture on the 12 pieces of rolled out dough.

Roll out the other 12 pieces of dough for the tops. Take water and using your fingers, wet around the edges of the bottom dough. Lay the top dough over the scrambled eggs and seal around the edge with a fork. Bake until golden brown.

Garnish with finely shredded cheddar cheese sprinkled on top of the pastelitos as they come out of the oven. Perfect served with green chili.

This recipe came from Jane Hude who has been with the Abriendo Inn for 8 years. She spent her early childhood years on a ranch in Montana. Her mother would fix pastelitos for the hands. When they were too busy to sit down for breakfast, they could grab a pastelito to eat while they were on horseback.

Temperature: 350 degrees
Cooking time: 30 minutes
  or until golden brown
Yield: 12 little pies

Pastry-
 3 cups flour
 1 teaspoon baking powder
 1 teaspoon salt
 2/3 cup shortening
 1 cup cold milk

Egg Mixture-
 6 eggs
 1 cup milk
 1 teaspoon salt
 1 pound chorizo sausage
 3/4 cup green onions, chopped (including the tops)
 1/3 cup green pepper, chopped
 1/3 cup red pepper, chopped
 3 tablespoons minced fresh cilantro

Rhubarb Crumble

Temperature: 350 degrees
Cooking time: 45 minutes
Yields: 12 to 16 servings

Crust-
  1 cup quick oatmeal
  1 cup brown sugar
  Pinch of salt
  1 cup flour
  1 cup margarine

Filling-
  4 cups diced rhubarb
   (about 10 stalks)
  1 can cherry pie filling
  1 cup water
  1 cup sugar
  2 tablespoons cornstarch
  ½ cup chopped
   almonds, slivered

Preheat the oven to 350 degrees. Mix the oatmeal, brown sugar, salt, flour and margarine, until crumbly. Press half the mixture into the bottom of a 9 x 13-inch pan. Layer the diced rhubarb on top of the crust. Boil together the sugar, cornstarch and water, until thick. Add the pie filling and stir. Spread over the rhubarb. Sprinkle the remaining crust mixture over the top. Sprinkle the almonds over the crust. Bake for 45 minutes. Top with whipped cream or non-dairy whipped topping of your choice.

Sticky Buns

Mix the brown sugar and milk; put in bottom of a greased bundt pan. Separate the buttermilk biscuits (do not use Grand Buttermilk biscuits) and set on end in the bundt pan. Mix the remaining ingredients together and spread over the buttermilk biscuits.

Bake at 350 degrees for 30 minutes. Let rest 15 minutes and invert onto serving platter.

"What a charming place! Everything was cozy, comfortable and perfect. We'll be back!"

Chris and Erika
Lubbock, Texas

Temperature: 350 degrees
Cooking time: 30 minutes
Yields: 24 rolls

$\frac{1}{2}$ **cup brown sugar**
3 tablespoons milk
3 packages buttermilk biscuits
$\frac{3}{4}$ **cup white sugar**
2 tablespoons cinnamon
1 stick of butter, melted

White Chocolate Raspberry Bars

Temperature: 325 degrees
Cooking time: 45 minutes
Yields: 24 bars

1 cup butter
4 cups white chocolate
** chips**
5 eggs
1 cup sugar
2 ¼ cups flour
1 teaspoon salt
1 tablespoon almond
** extract**
1 ¼ cups raspberry
** jam**
¾ cup almonds, sliced

Preheat oven to 325 degrees. Grease and flour a 9 x 13-inch pan. Melt the butter in a medium saucepan. Remove from heat and add the white chocolate chips. Let stand, but do not stir.

Beat the eggs in a large bowl. Add the sugar, continuing to beat. Stir in the melted white chocolate chips. Add the flour, salt and almond extract. Stir just until mixed. Spread half of the batter in the bottom of the pan. Bake for 15 minutes until light brown.

While the batter is baking in the oven, melt the raspberry jam in a small pan over low heat. Remove the baked bottom from the oven and spread the melted jam over the top. Spoon the remaining batter over the top of the jam. Sprinkle with sliced almonds. Return the pan to the oven and bake an additional 20 to 25 minutes or until golden brown. Let cool completely. Cut into bars prior to serving.

"White chocolate and raspberries together are wonderful."

Breakfast

Apple Cranberry Crisp with Maple Whipped Cream

Mix the first 6 ingredients together in a bowl. Add the butter and cut in until the mixture resembles coarse meal. Mix in the walnuts. Preheat the oven to 375 degrees. Combine the apples, cranberries, $1/3$ cup sugar and lemon juice in a bowl. Toss gently. Transfer to a buttered 12 cup baking dish. Sprinkle the topping over all. Cover with foil and cook 20 minutes. Uncover and bake until the apples are tender and the topping is golden brown, about 40 minutes. Spoon into bowls. Top with a dollop of maple whipped cream and fresh mint leaf.

For maple whipped cream, simply beat whipping cream and maple syrup together to the desired consistency.

"Never have we experienced a room with a more spectacular view. This is the perfect way to relax. The cookies and hot cider were just what we needed after a day of snowshoeing!"

Kathy & John
Denver, Colorado

Temperature: 375 degrees
Cooking time: 70 minutes
Yields: 6 servings

- **1 cup rolled oats**
- **$3/4$ cup flour**
- **$3/4$ cup brown sugar, packed**
- **1 teaspoon cinnamon**
- **$1/2$ teaspoon salt**
- **$1/4$ teaspoon nutmeg**
- **1 stick butter, cut into pieces**
- **$3/4$ cup walnuts, toasted**
- **10 large tart green apples, peeled, cored and cut into $1/4$-inch thick slices**
- **1 $1/3$ cups cranberries**
- **$1/3$ cup sugar**
- **2 tablespoons fresh lemon juice**

Fruit and Nut Granola

Temperature: 350 degrees
Cooking time: 20 to 30
  minutes
Yields: 12 cups
Can be stored for one
  month in an airtight
  container.

4 cups old fashioned
  rolled oats
2 cups sweetened,
  shredded coconut
2 cups sliced almonds
¾ cup vegetable oil
½ cup honey
1 ½ cups dried apricots
1 cup dried figs
1 cup dried cherries
1 cup roasted, unsalted
  cashews

Toss oats, coconut and almonds together in a large bowl. Whisk together oil and honey in a small bowl. Pour the oil mixture over the oat mixture. Stir with a wooden spoon until mixture is coated. Spread onto a 13 x 18 x 3-inch baking sheet. Bake in a preheated 350 degree oven, stirring occasionally, for approximately 20 to 30 minutes or until golden brown.

Remove pan from oven and stir until cool. Add remaining ingredients.

"A lovely home and a completely romantic room. Too bad I was alone and on a business trip. Hope to return someday with my wonderful husband. Cheers!"

Barbara
Fort Worth, TX

Giddy-up Grits

Brown the sausage and drain. Add the Tabasco™ sauce, garlic salt and pepper to sausage; set aside. Cook the grits in the boiling water. Add all the ingredients together. Stir until well mixed.

Pour the mixture into a well buttered baking dish. Bake uncovered at 350 degrees for 1 hour.

Garnish with chopped cilantro, red bell peppers and sour cream.

This recipe has been featured in Sunset Magazine.

Temperature: 350 degrees
Cooking time: 1 hour
Yields: 6 servings

1 pound sausage
1 teaspoon Tabasco™ sauce (to taste)
Garlic to taste
¾ teaspoon pepper
1 cup instant grits
4 cups boiling water
2 cups extra sharp cheese, grated
¼ cup butter, melted
2 large eggs, well beaten
1, 8-ounce can mild green chilies, seeded and chopped

Irish Potato Pancakes

Temperature: griddle, 375 degrees
Yields: 10 servings

1 green pepper
1 red pepper
1 onion
1 tablespoon salt
½ teaspoon black pepper
8 cups shredded white potatoes, thawed to room temperature
6 eggs
1 cup flour
1 cup Half & Half™
1 teaspoon garlic, minced
Olive and canola oil

Chop the onions and peppers, then sauté lightly in olive oil. Set aside. In a large mixing bowl, combine the eggs, Half & Half™, black pepper, garlic and salt. Whisk well. Add the flour and mix. Add the onion and peppers mixture. Add the potatoes and mix together thoroughly.

Pre-heat a frying pan or griddle to 375 degrees and brush with the canola oil. Spoon out the mixture onto the griddle, forming them into 6 to 7-inch diameter cakes. Flip the cakes over, frying each side. Sample the first cake for salt content. Typically you add more salt to potato dishes than you might normally think. Serve the pancakes topped with sour cream and finely chopped green onions. Add more sour cream on the side

Morning Fruit Crisp

Spread fruit in the bottom of a 7 x 11-inch lightly greased pan. Mix dry ingredients together. Mix the egg into the dry ingredients to form a mixture with a crumbled texture and sprinkle over the fruit. Drizzle melted butter over crumb topping.

Bake at 350 degrees for 25 to 30 minutes or until the top is golden brown and the fruit bubbles. Garnish with whipped cream, ice cream, or milk. Serve warm for a breakfast dessert.

"This Inn has more charm than a love story written for entertainment."

Daniel & Victoria
Fort Worth, TX

Temperature: 350 degrees
Cooking time: 25 to 30
  minutes
Yields: 6 to 8 servings

  1 cup all-purpose flour
  1 cup sugar
  ½ cup oats (quick or
    old fashioned) optional
  2 teaspoons baking
    powder
  1 egg
  2 tablespoons melted
    butter
  2 cups of fruit, such as
    apples, peaches, cherry
    pie filling, blueberry
    pie filling, canned
    pineapple tidbits with
    sliced bananas

Peach Raspberry Oatmeal Crisp

Temperature: 375 degrees
Cooking time: 45 minutes
Yields: 10 to 12 servings

Fruit-
  6 large fresh peaches,
    sliced
  ½ cup sugar
  ½ teaspoon cinnamon
  ½ pint raspberries

Topping-
  3 cups oatmeal
  ⅓ cup flour
  ¾ cup brown sugar
  ½ cup butter, melted
  ½ teaspoon cinnamon
  ¼ teaspoon nutmeg
  ½ cup pecans
    (optional)

Grease and flour a 9 x 13-inch pan. In a bowl, combine the sliced peaches, sugar and cinnamon. Evenly coat the peaches and place them on the bottom of the prepared pan. Sprinkle with raspberries. Mix together all the topping ingredients and spread evenly over the fruit. Bake for 30 to 35 minutes.

Serve immediately.

"As we prepare to depart this lovely room, we want to express our great pleasure of having experienced the comfort and serenity which is exuded throughout the house. Too bad we must return to 'reality'! We look forward to our next visit with anticipation. Since we live in the area, we will enjoy the memory of our first visit each time we pass this wonderful place. Thanks!"

Cheryl & Mark
Fort Collins/Longmont, CO

Rhonda's Rummy Starter

Roast the chopped pecans in the oven for about 10 minutes at 425 degrees. Set aside. This can be done in advance. Slice bananas peaches and pears lengthwise. You can use one or all fruits, in whatever quantity you want to serve. Melt a dab of butter in a non-stick skillet. Add the fruit to the skillet and sprinkle with brown sugar and cinnamon. Turn fruit carefully and sprinkle with more brown sugar and cinnamon, adding a little lemon juice. Watch carefully to avoid over cooking. When the fruit is slightly golden, add a dash of rum to the pan, swirling the pan around until the rum evaporates.

Serve on plates dusted with powdered sugar. Place a warmed slice of pound cake on plate, arranging the fruit on top (artfully) then drizzle with Romanoff sauce. Whip the cream and place a dollop of whipped cream on the side. Sprinkle with toasted pecans.

Temperature: stovetop, medium
Cooking time: 25 minutes
Sauce can be stored up to 1 week

Unsalted butter
Bananas, fresh peaches or fresh pears, depending upon the season
Brown sugar
Cinnamon
Lemon juice
Rum
Pecans, chopped
Whipping cream
Packaged pound cake

Romanoff Sauce

Yields: 1 ½ cups
Stores for up to 1 week in the refrigerator

1 ½ cups dairy sour cream
2 tablespoons powdered sugar
2 tablespoons brown sugar
1 tablespoon dark rum
1 teaspoon shredded orange peel
½ teaspoon ground cinnamon
½ teaspoon ground nutmeg

Mix the ingredients together. Cover and refrigerate for up to one week, but a minimum of 24 hours.

Use this sauce to drizzle over the top of Rhonda's Rummy Starter.

"I just love dessert for breakfast, the combination of pears & bananas are so delicious & unique. We will be back for more next year!"

Ted and Nancy Gaouette

Artichoke Bacon Frittata

Preheat the oven to 325 degrees. In a skillet, sauté the chopped onion in butter until transparent. Add the artichokes along with the liquid from one jar. Heat for 2 minutes, stirring. In a bowl, lightly beat the eggs. Add the cheese, bread crumbs, artichoke mixture and bacon. Mix together and place in greased 9-inch quiche pan or 6 greased ramekins. Bake for 25 minutes, until set. Sprinkle the frittata with the Monterey Jack cheese, if desired, and bake for 5 more minutes. Serve immediately topped with fresh sliced Roma tomatoes and sour cream.

"Hospitality is a gift and yours is shared so gracefully. The worth and special moments of this wedding night are framed in a beautiful memory of this inn and the gracious hospitality of its hosts."

Dale and Jan
California

Temperature: 325 degrees
Cooking time: 30 minutes
Yields: 6 servings

1 small onion, chopped
2 tablespoons butter
2, 6 ½-ounce jars marinated artichoke hearts, drained and chopped (reserve liquid from 1 jar)
6 eggs
⅓ cup grated Parmesan cheese
⅓ cup bread crumbs
6 slices bacon, cooked and crumbled
½ cup shredded Monterey Jack cheese (optional)
4 Roma tomatoes, sliced thin
Sour cream

Cloud City Casserole

Temperature: 350 degrees
Cooking time: 45 to 60
  minutes
Yields: 8 to 10 servings

6 large eggs
2 cups milk
2 cups seasoned bread
  cubes
1 cup shredded cheese
  (Cheddar, Swiss,
  Monterey Jack or com-
  bination)
1 pound cooked loose
  sausage
½ teaspoon dry
  mustard
Salt, pepper, basil,
  cilantro to taste
½ cup mushrooms,
  sliced
¼ cup black olives,
  sliced
½ cup broccoli pieces
½ cup carrots,
  shredded

Start the night before you want to serve the dish. Beat the eggs until fluffy. Add in the milk, dry mustard and cheese. Butter a 9 x 13-inch pan or two 7 x 11-inch pans. Sprinkle bread cubes on the bottom of pan. Pour the liquid mixture carefully over the cubes. Arrange the vegetables on top. Cover with plastic wrap and refrigerate overnight.

The next morning bake at 350 degrees (no need to pre-heat) for 30 minutes. In the meantime, cook and drain the sausage in a skillet. Sprinkle sausage over the casserole and return to the oven for an additional 15 to 30 minutes. Garnish with sour cream or spinach sauce or hollandaise.

"We have traveled across the world after seeing the web site and it was worth the trip!!"

Roger & Cardine
Amsterdam, The Netherlands

Country Quiche

In a mixing bowl, whisk the eggs and sour cream. Add any or all of the optional ingredients in small quantities; set aside.

In a separate mixing bowl, mix the flour and salt; cut in the margarine with a fork. Add water and toss mixture using the fork until the flour is moist. Form into a ball and roll out onto a floured surface. Place the pie crust in a pie pan. Pour the quiche mix into the pie crust. Bake uncovered at 375 degrees for approximately 50 minutes until quiche is brown on top and puffs up.

This quiche is served during our Bed & Breakfast season and is complemented well with a side dish of fresh fruit and a large glass of orange juice.

"Thank you very much for the great food and accommodations! The German Chocolate cake was our favorite! We'll definitely be back again and again!"

Temperature: 375 degrees
Cooking time: 50 minutes
Yields: 8 servings

Quiche-
  5 large eggs
  1, 16 ounce container
    sour cream

Optional Ingredients-
  Cheese
  Ham
  Bacon
  Onion
  Green peppers
  Mushrooms

Pie Crust-
  1 $\frac{1}{4}$ cups flour
  $\frac{1}{4}$ teaspoon salt
  $\frac{1}{3}$ cup margarine
  4 to 5 tablespoons cold
    water

Crustless Crab Meat Quiche

Temperature: 350 degrees
Cooking time: 45 minutes
Yields: 8 servings

8 ounces of crabmeat
8 ounces of fresh
  mushrooms, sliced
2 tablespoons butter
4 eggs
1 cup sour cream
1 cup small-curd cottage
  cheese
1/2 cup grated Parmesan
cheese
1/4 cup flour
1 teaspoon onion
  powder
1/4 teaspoon salt
4 drops hot pepper
  sauce
2 cups (8 ounces)
  Monterey Jack cheese,
  shredded

In a medium skillet, sauté the mushrooms in butter until tender. Remove mushrooms with a slotted spoon and drain on paper towels.

In a blender or food processor fitted with a steel blade, blend eggs, sour cream, cottage cheese, Parmesan cheese, flour, onion powder, salt and hot pepper sauce. Fold in mushrooms, jack cheese and crabmeat. Pour into a 10-inch porcelain quiche dish or 9 1/2-inch deep-dish pie plate. Bake in a preheated 350-degree oven for 45 minutes or until a knife inserted near the center comes out clean. The quiche should be puffed and golden brown. Let stand 5 minutes before cutting into wedges.

Ham and Mushroom Strata

In a medium saucepan, sauté the garlic and onion in butter for 5 minutes. Mix in flour. Add broth gradually, stirring and allowing the sauce to thicken between additions. When half of the broth has been added, stir in sherry, nutmeg, dry mustard, salt and pepper. When all the broth has been added, remove from heat and allow to cool for 10 minutes. Beat together sour cream and eggs in a bowl. Add to the partially cooled sauce.

Sauté the mushrooms in butter for 10 minutes. Grease a 9 x 13-inch baking dish. Spread the bread cubes along the bottom. Lay the ham cubes and sautéed mushroom slices on top of the bread cubes. Sprinkle with Swiss and Parmesan cheese. Pour egg mixture over all ingredients in the baking dish. Cover with plastic wrap and refrigerate overnight.

In the morning, preheat the oven to 350 degrees. Bake the strata for 45 to 50 minutes or until puffed and golden. Serve hot.

This is a perfect way to use leftover bread. Make this dish the night before and wake up to a gourmet breakfast.

Temperature: 350 degrees
Cooking time: 45 to 50
** minutes**
Yields: 8 servings

Sauce-
  $1/4$ cup butter
  1 clove garlic, minced
  $1/2$ cup onion, chopped
  $1/4$ cup flour
  2 $1/2$ cups chicken or
    vegetable broth
  $1/4$ cup sherry
  $1/8$ teaspoon nutmeg
  $1/4$ teaspoon dry
    mustard
  Salt and pepper to taste
  1 cup sour cream
  16 eggs

Assembly-
  1 loaf of French bread,
    fresh or stale, cubed
  1 pound of mushrooms,
    sliced
  2 tablespoons butter
  1 pound ham, cubed
  2 cups Swiss cheese,
    grated
  $1/2$ cup freshly grated
    Parmesan cheese

John Wayne Casserole

Temperature: 325 degrees
Cooking time: 45 to 60
   minutes
Yields: 8 servings

1 tablespoon butter
8 eggs, separated
20 ounces sour cream
$\frac{1}{2}$ cup whole milk
4 cups Monterrey Jack
   and mild Cheddar
   cheese
$\frac{1}{2}$ teaspoon garlic,
   minced
$\frac{1}{2}$ teaspoon black
   pepper
1 small red pepper
1 small green pepper
1 onion
1 Anaheim pepper
1 $\frac{1}{2}$ cups flour
Olive oil, extra virgin
1 tomato, thinly sliced
   for topping
Diced ham or cooked
   Canadian bacon
   (optional)

Preheat the oven to 325 degrees. Chop the onion and peppers, then sauté lightly in the olive oil; set aside. In a large mixing bowl, separate the egg yolks from the whites, leaving the yolks in the bowl. Add milk, flour, garlic and black pepper to the yolks, and then mix well. Add sour cream, the cheeses and the vegetable mixture.

In another mixing bowl, beat the egg whites until stiff. Fold the beaten whites into the mixture in the other bowl and blend together. Grease a baking dish with butter. Pour the mixture into the baking dish and place in the hot oven. Bake for 45 to 60 minutes, turning the dish occasionally, until the top starts to crack. Three quarters of the way through baking top with the tomato slices.

Serve with apple cinnamon tortillas slathered with honey butter.

Olde Miner's Breakfast

Scrub potatoes and cut into thumb-sized pieces. Cook in small amount of water until just barely tender. Drain thoroughly. May be cooked the night before.

Lightly sauté the peppers and onions until they just begin to become translucent. Lightly sauté the mushrooms separately. Drain.

Place the potatoes in a large, greased baking pan. Add the chopped fresh basil leaves. Sprinkle with salt, pepper, garlic and Fines Herbs; toss. Add sautéed vegetables and spinach (ham if desired). Tuck the spinach down so it doesn't stick up. Roast uncovered, until lightly browned, 30 to 60 minutes.

Place serving on salad sized plate. Lightly cover with grated cheddar cheese. Melt on second shelf under the broiler for about 5 minutes.

Garnish with a dollop of sour cream and olives. Top with parsley sprig or chives.

Temperature: 350 degrees
Cooking time: 30 to 60
** minutes**
Yields: 20 servings

10 pounds potatoes
2 cups red peppers,
** largely diced**
2 cups onions, largely
** diced**
1 pound mushrooms,
** largely sliced**
Fresh spinach, washed,
** dried thoroughly and**
** chopped coarsely**
Chopped ham (optional)
Salt
Pepper
Garlic
Fines herbs
Cheddar cheese, grated
Parsley
Sour cream
Several stalks fresh basil
** leaves, chopped**
Olives

Quiche Lorraine

Temperature: 375 degrees
Cooking time: 45 to 50
  minutes
Yields: 4 to 6 servings

4 to 5 strips bacon
1 onion, sliced thin
1 cup Swiss cheese,
  shredded
¼ cup Parmesan cheese
4 eggs
¼ teaspoon salt
¼ teaspoon white
  pepper
1 ⅓ cups whipping
  cream
9-inch prepared pie
  shell, unbaked
¼ cup parsley, chopped
Fresh fruit in season

Fry the bacon until crisp; reserve a portion of the grease. Drain the bacon strips well on paper towels and crumble. Sauté the onion in the reserved bacon grease until transparent. Layer the onion in the bottom of the unbaked pie shell; top with the cheeses, then bacon. Mix together the eggs, salt, pepper and cream; pour into pie shell. Bake at 375 degrees for 45 to 50 minutes until set. Garnish with the chopped parsley. Serve with fresh fruit.

"I've seen some of the best B & B's any-where and the St. Elmo is one of them! Excellent attention to detail. Thank you for a weekend that began as a stress-breaker and became a second honeymoon."

Quiche to Die For

Line each pie shell with 1 cup of cheese. Sprinkle 1 cup of the mixed vegetables into each shell. Beat the eggs, spices and flour together in a separate bowl. Beat the milk into the egg mixture. Divide and pour equally over the 3 prepared shells. Bake for 60 minutes or until the custard is firm to the touch. Garnish with some white cheese and bake an additional 15 minutes.

Serve with fresh fruits and fried or scalloped potatoes.

Temperature: 375 degrees
Cooking time: 75 minutes
Yields: 18 servings (3 pies)
Can be stored for 1 to 2
  days

3 cups Cheddar cheese,
  grated
3 cups vegetable mix
  (sliced mushrooms,
  chopped onion,
  chopped peppers,
  spinach)
12 eggs
$\frac{1}{2}$ teaspoon salt
$\frac{1}{2}$ teaspoon pepper
2 teaspoons herbs/spices
  of your choice
3 tablespoons flour
6 cups milk
3 unbaked pie shells

Salmon Frittata

Temperature: 375 degrees
Cooking time: 40 minutes
Yields: 6 servings

**1 medium yellow onion,
   chopped**
2 tablespoons butter
8 ounces cream cheese
**½ pound baked salmon
   filet or 6 ounces
   canned salmon, skin-
   less and boneless**
**1 tablespoon fresh
   lemon juice**
**2 Idaho or Russet
   potatoes**
6 eggs
1 cup milk
1 teaspoon dill
Salt and pepper to taste
Paprika

Sauté the onions in butter for 5 to 10 minutes, until translucent. Stir in the salmon and lemon juice; sauté 5 minutes. Peel and thinly slice the potatoes. Butter a 9-inch round baking dish. Line the bottom with potato slices. Cut the cream cheese into cubes and place on top of the potatoes. Spread the salmon mixture on top. Beat together the eggs, milk, dill, salt and pepper. Pour the egg mixture over the other ingredients in the baking dish. Sprinkle with the paprika. Bake at 375 degrees for about 40 minutes or until puffed and golden. Serve hot.

"This is a superb place with wonderful staff. Would we otherwise have traveled 5,000 miles to spend our fouth vacation here?"

Mechenheim, Germany

Sausage and Potato Strata

Brown the sausage, draining off the excess fat; crumble the meat. Spray a 9 x 13-inch baking dish with non-stick vegetable oil spray and place the sausage in the dish. Sauté the potatoes in butter with onion, until golden. Layer the potatoes over the sausage, and then sprinkle with cheese. If you are preparing ahead of time, this is the point where you may stop and refrigerate, until needed for use.

Beat the eggs and milk together. Add the salt and pepper. Pour over the sausage and potatoes in the baking dish. Bake in 350 degree oven for 45 to 50 minutes or until set. A knife inserted into the middle should come out clean. Serve with English muffins or croissants.

Temperature: 350 degrees
Cooking time: 45 to 50 minutes
Yields: 8 servings

1 pound lean sausage
3 tablespoons butter
6 eggs, beaten
1 cup Swiss, Monterey Jack or Cheddar cheese, grated
¾ cup onion, chopped
4 large frozen hash brown squares
Pepper to taste
2 ½ cups milk
½ teaspoon salt

Spinach Feta Quiche

Temperature: 325 degrees
Cooking time: 35 to 40 minutes
Yields: 6 servings
Can be stored overnight

1 tablespoon butter
1 small onion, chopped
¼ cup fresh parsley, chopped
1 teaspoon dill
1 teaspoon basil
10 ounces frozen chopped spinach, thawed and dried
3 tablespoons milk
4 ounces Feta cheese, crumbled
1 ½ cups Swiss cheese, shredded
Pinch of nutmeg
Salt and pepper to taste
3 eggs, separated
9-inch pie shell, unbaked

Sauté the onion in butter until transparent. Add the herbs and sauté until wilted. Combine the onion and herb mixture with spinach, lemon juice, milk, cheese, nutmeg, salt and pepper. Mix well. Separate the eggs and stir the yolks into the spinach mixture.

Beat the egg whites to stiff peaks and gently fold into spinach mixture. Pour into the pie shell and bake at 325 degrees for 35 to 40 minutes or until quiche is puffed and slightly browned.

"What a model of grace and rest. From the cookies & milk downstairs to the heart-shaped pillows, you had here everything we could have asked for. It all felt as welcoming as a visit to grandma's—only grandma was about 40 years old and had impeccable taste! 'Twas a perfect site for a first night of marriage. Thanks for the champagne & everything else. We'll remember this always! Thanks!"

Floyd & Lila

Baked Omelette Sandwich

Spray a 9 x 13-inch glass baking dish with cooking spray. Line the bottom of the dish with bread slices. Layer Cheddar cheese, ham and Swiss cheese. Butter the remaining bread slices on one side and lay them atop the cheese and ham layer, buttered side up.

Mix the eggs, milk, dry mustard, onion and garlic powders together. Pour over the top of the bread. Refrigerate overnight before baking.

The next morning, sprinkle the crushed corn flake crumbs over the top and drizzle with 1/4 cup melted butter. Cover with foil sprayed with cooking spray and bake for 60 minutes at 350 degrees. Remove the foil during the last 15 minutes to brown. Let set 10 minutes before cutting. Garnish with chopped tomato and parsley.

"Thanks so much for the great getaway! Food was wonderful and the other guests charming. I'm looking forward to returning with my husband."

Mary Sue
Littleton, CO

Temperature: 350 degrees
Cooking time: 1 hour
Yields: 8 servings

16 to 20 slices English muffin bread, crusts trimmed off
2 packages deli ham, torn into pieces
1/2 pound Cheddar cheese, shredded
1/2 pound Swiss cheese (or Monterey Jack), shredded
8 eggs
3 cups milk
1/2 teaspoon dry mustard
1/2 teaspoon onion powder
1/2 teaspoon garlic powder
1 1/2 cups corn flakes, crushed
1/4 cup butter, melted

Chili Egg Puff

Temperature: 350 degrees
Cooking time: 55 minutes
Yields: 8 servings

14 whole eggs
½ cup flour
1 teaspoon baking soda
½ teaspoon salt
½ teaspoon pepper
½ teaspoon nutmeg
1 ½ teaspoons Dijon
   mustard (Grey
   Poupon™)
1 pint large curd cottage
   cheese
1 pound Monterrey Jack
   cheese, shredded
½ cup butter, melted
4 ounces diced green
   chilies

Beat the eggs together. Add the other ingredients and mix well. Pour into a well greased glass baking dish. Bake at 350 degrees for 55 minutes. Remove from the oven and let stand for 10 minutes. Serve with salsa on the side.

Egg Asparagus Breakfast Burritos

Preheat the oven to 375 degrees. Warm the tortillas in a microwave. Snap, scale and cook the asparagus in boiling water, until cooked, but not limp. Toss with lemon juice. Scramble the eggs with the pepper. Place 3 asparagus spears, $\frac{1}{8}$ of the egg and $\frac{1}{8}$ of the cheese in the middle of each tortilla. Roll and place in a baking dish. Cover and bake 20 minutes or until the tortillas are slightly crisp on the ends. Garnish with slices of orange.

These are a nice, light breakfast.

Temperature: 375 degrees
Cooking time: 20 minutes
Yields: 4 servings

8, 6-inch flour tortillas
24 pieces of fresh
  asparagus
1 tablespoon lemon juice
5 eggs
Pinch of pepper
$\frac{1}{3}$ cup skim milk
1 tablespoon chives,
  minced
$\frac{1}{4}$ teaspoon lemon rind
$\frac{1}{2}$ cup Monterey Jack
  cheese, shredded
Orange for garnish

"I can't describe in writing what our stay with you meant to us. It was one of the most enjoyable things we have ever done as a family. We are in love with your ranch and the people that make it special. We will be back!!"

John & Carrie
Hudson, WI

Eggs in Bacon Baskets

**Temperature: 350 degrees
 in a convection oven
Cooking time: 15 minutes
Yields: 4 servings**

**8 bacon strips
6 eggs
2 cups Half & Half™
Paprika
3 green onions, chopped
½ cup Cheddar cheese,
 shredded**

Fry or microwave bacon until it is crisp. Spray vegetable oil into the muffin tins. While it is warm, place the bacon in a muffin tin to mold it into a circle. This may be done the night before. Store the cooled bacon circles in the refrigerator.

Break an egg into each muffin tin in the center of the bacon. Top each egg with 1 to 1 ½ table-spoons of Half & Half™. Dust with salt and pepper. Sprinkle paprika over each egg.

Bake for 14 minutes or until the egg yolk is set. Top the egg with green onions and Cheddar cheese. Return the eggs to the oven until the cheese has melted. Serve immediately.

Can be served with salsa or fresh fruit.

"You should feel very pleased with the countless things you have perfected in a short amount of time. From the attention to details, to the wonderful hospitality, to the granola and hot entrees in the morning, this experience will be one we cherish. Thank you for this magical retreat."

*Jeff and Julie
Washington*

Eggs Southwest

Preheat oven to 350 degrees. Butter 8 individual ramekins (8 ounce size). Divide ingredients evenly between all 8 ramekins. Place 2 tablespoons of the enchilada sauce into the bottom of each ramekin. Layer the ground sausage and crumbled cornbread. Make 2 spaces and drop 2 eggs into each dish, being careful not to break the yolks. Sprinkle with the Cheddar cheese. Top with a slice of tomato.

Bake until the eggs appear firm, but not hard and cheese is bubbly. Place the ramekin on a plate; garnish with a dollop of sour cream, guacamole and sprigs of cilantro.

"Suzy, your Eggs Southwest were just the prefect touch to our Colorado visit! Would you come home with us?"

Jeri and Leland Ross
New York, NY

Temperature: 350 degrees
Cooking time: 10 to 12
  minutes
Yields: 8 servings

1 pound ground sausage,
  lightly fried, & drained
  (can be done the day
  before)
2 cups Cheddar cheese,
  shredded
Cornbread recipe
1 can (16 ounces) green
  chili enchilada sauce (I
  use Hatch™ brand)
16 eggs
Butter
2 tomatoes, sliced
Cilantro
Guacamole
Sour cream

Oven Baked Eggs

Temperature: 350 degrees
Cooking time: 1 hour
Yields: 7 to 8 servings

4 slices of bread, cubed,
  crust removed
1 cup milk
5 eggs, well beaten
½ teaspoon dry
  mustard
½ teaspoon salt
1 cup Cheddar cheese,
  shredded
1 ½ tablespoons onion,
  finely diced

Preheat the oven to 350 degrees. Place the bread in the bottom of a greased 9 x 13-inch pan. Beat together the eggs, milk, mustard and salt. Stir in the onions and cheese. Pour the mix over the top of the bread. Place in oven and bake for 1 hour or until golden brown. Garnish with cheese and parsley.

Serve with sausage links, hash browns and homemade cinnamon rolls for a hearty ranch breakfast.

Oven Baked Omelette

Spray a 9-inch pie pan with a non-stick cooking spray. Whip together the eggs, cottage cheese, sour cream and chives in a medium bowl. Spread the salsa over the bottom of the pan and sprinkle the cheeses over the salsa. Pour the egg mixture over the cheeses. Bake in a 350 degree oven for 45 minutes.

Temperature: 350 degrees
Cooking time: 45 minutes
Yields: 4 to 6 servings

6 eggs
$\frac{1}{2}$ cup cottage cheese
$\frac{1}{2}$ cup sour cream
$\frac{1}{2}$ cup salsa
1 cup Monterey Jack or Mozzarella cheese, shredded
1 cup Cheddar cheese, shredded
1 tablespoon chives, chopped

"What a marvelous evening—a marvelous place—to celebrate rest. This rates as our best Colorado B & B memory (of the three we've stayed in) and the best of others across the country. We appreciated the fine detailing and appointments of this B & B, best of any we've seen. Someone sure pays attention to that and it makes a difference."

Bill and Kathleen

Sherried Breakfast Cups

Temperature: 400 degrees
Cooking time: 35 minutes
Yields: 8 servings

- 8 Pepperidge Farm™ pastry shells
- 3 tablespoons butter, plus ½ teaspoon butter
- 8 ounces mushrooms, sliced
- 1 medium onion, finely chopped
- 2 tablespoons flour
- ½ teaspoon dried chives
- ¼ teaspoon salt
- ¼ teaspoon black pepper
- ½ teaspoon thyme
- ¼ cup sour cream
- 1 tablespoon dry cooking sherry
- 8 eggs
- 2 tablespoons water
- Monterey Jack cheese, shredded

Preheat oven to 400 decrees. Bake the pastry shells according to the instructions on the box. Remove from oven and while still warm remove the shells lids and set aside. The shells can be baked ahead of time and stored at room temperature.

In a large sauté pan melt 3 tablespoons butter on medium-high heat. Add the mushrooms and onion; sauté until the onions are cooked through, approximately 5 minutes. Add the flour and spices. Turn off the heat and stir well. Add the sour cream and sherry. Mix well to blend all ingredients; set aside in bowl.

Add ½ teaspoon butter to the same pan and melt on medium heat. Whisk together the eggs and waler; pour into the pan and scramble, just until the eggs begin to set, but are still soft. Fold in the mushroom mixture, making sure all ingredients are combined. Remove from heat.

Place the baked pastry shells on individual serving plates; divide the egg/mushroom mixture evenly between the shells, overflowing each. Sprinkle cheese over top of each and place plates in oven just until cheese melts. Remove plates from oven and place the pastry shells' lids on top of the melted cheese. Garnish with fresh parsley and serve with bacon slices.

Swiss Onion Eggs

In a large frying pan over medium heat melt 2 tablespoons butter. Add the onions; cook slowly, stirring often until onion is limp and tender (about 30 minutes). Melt the remaining 1 tablespoon butter in a small saucepan over medium heat. Stir in the flour and cook until bubbly. Gradually stir in the milk and cook, stirring constantly, until thick and smooth. Stir in the mustard, salt, parsley and pepper. In individual ramekins layer onions, eggs (sliced), cheese and white sauce. Refrigerate overnight.

The next morning, bake at 375 degrees for 40 minutes or until bubbly. Garnish with the chopped parsley. Serve with fresh fruit.

Temperature: 375 degrees
Cooking time: 40 minutes
Yields: 6 servings
Can be stored overnight
  in refrigerator

3 tablespoons butter
2 large onions, thinly
  sliced, separated into
  rings
1 tablespoon flour
1 cup milk
½ teaspoon Dijon
  mustard
½ teaspoon salt
2 teaspoons parsley,
  chopped
¼ teaspoon white
  pepper
6 hard boiled eggs
2 cups Swiss cheese,
  shredded
¼ cup fresh parsley,
  chopped
Fresh fruit in season

Apple Butter Pancakes

Temperature: 325 degrees
Cooking time: 4 to 8
  minutes
Yields: 5 servings

2 cups flour
2 teaspoons baking
  powder
1 teaspoon baking soda
1 teaspoon salt
4 tablespoons sugar
2 cups milk
6 tablespoons apple
  butter
4 tablespoons butter,
  melted
2 eggs

Garnish-
  Toasted pine nuts
  Powdered sugar
  Dollop of apple butter

Preheat the griddle to 325 degrees. Combine the dry ingredients; set aside. Combine the wet ingredients in a separate bowl. If the milk is cold, warm it in the microwave so the melted butter won't solidify. Be careful not to have the milk hot, as it will cook the eggs! Mix the wet ingredients into the dry ingredients.

Use ⅓ cup measure to spoon pancakes out onto griddle. Cook until lightly browned and fluffy looking. Cooking time can vary due to how large you make the pancakes. I use molds in various shapes that are available through gourmet cooking shops.

Garnish with toasted pine nuts, apple butter and powdered sugar. I also serve two strips of bacon on the side.

"I never knew pancakes could be so divine!"

Marcy and Michael DeLand

Apple Lemon Pancakes

Peel, core and coarsely shred the apple; set aside. Combine the flour, sugar, baking powder, soda and salt. In a separate bowl combine the eggs, milk and melted butter. Add the shredded apple and lemon peel. Add to the flour mixture. Mix well. Cook the pancakes on a medium-hot griddle. Garnish with fresh berries and serve 3 pancakes per person with blueberry or raspberry syrup. Serve with sausage or bacon on the side.

Yields: 6 servings
Can be stored overnight

1 medium apple
2 cups flour
2 tablespoons sugar
2 teaspoons baking powder
$\frac{1}{4}$ teaspoon baking soda
$\frac{1}{8}$ teaspoon salt
2 eggs, lightly beaten
1 $\frac{2}{3}$ cups milk
2 tablespoons butter, melted
1 tablespoon lemon peel, finely shredded
Blueberry or raspberry syrup
Fresh raspberries or blueberries
Sausage or bacon

Briar Rose Award Winning Crepes

Cooking time: 1 to 2
minutes
Yields: 10 crepes
Can be stored overnight
in an airtight container

¼ cup all-purpose flour
½ cup whole wheat
flour
1 ¼ cups milk
1 egg plus 1 egg yolk
1 tablespoon of melted
butter or oil

Place all the ingredients in a blender and run at high speed for 10 to 15 seconds. Scrape down the sides and run again for 5 to 10 seconds. Batter may be used immediately. Heat a crepe pan. Ladle a small amount of the batter (¾ to 1 ounce, depending upon pan size) into the crepe pan. Tilt the pan to spread the batter evenly over its surface. Cook until the bubbles open and the crepe starts to brown near the edges. Turn the crepe to brown on the other side. Remove and place on paper towels until ready to use. You can use either the Banana Filling or B & B Melba Sauce to fill the finished crepes.

Garnish with an orange slice, lemon peel curl, mint leaf, whipped cream or whipped butter. Can be served as a rich breakfast treat or as a dessert. When served as a dessert, a small drizzle of chocolate sauce or shaved chocolate makes a wonderful garnish. Or, combine with vanilla ice cream.

AWARD WINNER

B & B Melba Sauce

Place the thawed raspberries in a blender and puree at high speed for 10 to 15 seconds. Strain the puree through a sieve fine enough to remove the seeds, and then pour into a saucepan. Add the sugar, lemon juice, and B & B liqueur to the saucepan and bring the liquid just to a boil. Add the cornstarch/water mixture. Stir a few minutes, until thickened. May be made ahead and refrigerated or used warm. Cover the center of a 10 or 12-inch plate with a thin layer of Melba sauce. Arrange 1 or 2 filled crepes on the plate, and pour additional Melba sauce over the crepes. May be garnished with lemon peel curl or a small rosette of whipped cream.

This makes a delicious sundae sauce on vanilla ice cream.

Cooking time: 4 to 5 minutes
Yields: 6 or more servings
Can be refrigerated for several weeks

12 ounces frozen raspberries, thawed
3 tablespoons sugar or more to taste
Juice of ½ lemon or 1 tablespoon bottled lemon juice
1 ounce B & B™ liqueur
1 teaspoon cornstarch dissolved in 1 tablespoon cold water

"It is a gift to have such a warm home across the street from where my daughter goes to school."

Deborah

Banana Filling

**Cooking time: 5 minutes
at most**
Yields: 4 to 6 servings

**4 to 6 ripe, firm bananas
(1 banana per serving)**
2 tablespoons butter
⅓ cup brown sugar
**2 tablespoons tart
orange or lemon
marmalade**
¼ teaspoon cinnamon
**¼ teaspoon almond
extract**
**¼ teaspoon vanilla
extract**
**1 ½ ounces B & B
liqueur**

Melt the butter in a fry pan or chafing dish over medium heat. Add the brown sugar and marmalade and allow them to melt completely. Cut the bananas in half lengthwise and across. Cook the bananas in the butter/sugar/marmalade mixture for 2 to 4 minutes, turning gently until they are just warm and soft. Add the extracts, B & B liqueur and sprinkle cinnamon over the entire mixture. Fold the mixture very gently so as not to break the bananas and remove from heat. Spoon (or spatula) banana mixture onto a warm crepe and fold or roll as desired.

This sauce can also be spooned over ice cream for a sumptuous desert.

"Once again time here was wonderful. Even with our busy life, we did relax and enjoy our fireplace room."

Denise

French Toast Casserole

Beat together all ingredients other than the bread, with a whisk, and set aside. Grease a 9 x 13-inch cake pan with butter. Cut French bread into $1/2$-inch thick slices and place each into the cake pan. Pour egg mixture over the bread slices. Cover and refrigerate overnight.

To bake, remove the cover, dot the bread with butter and sprinkle with cinnamon and sugar. Bake at 350 degrees for 55 minutes or until toast is light brown.

Serve with pure maple syrup, yogurt or sour cream and fruit.

Temperature: 350 degrees
Cooking time: 55 minutes
Yields: 8 to 10 servings

8 large eggs
3 cups milk
4 teaspoons sugar
$1/3$ teaspoon salt
1 tablespoon vanilla
1 teaspoon cinnamon
1 loaf French bread

"I MISS the ranch! I re-read your brochure as I put away stuff—you sure delivered on everything!"

Gingerbread Pancakes with Lemon Sauce

Temperature: stovetop,
medium
Yields: 10 pancakes

1 ½ cups all-purpose
flour
1 teaspoon baking
powder
1 teaspoon ground
cinnamon
½ teaspoon ground
ginger
¼ teaspoon baking
soda
¼ teaspoon salt
1 egg
1 ¼ cups milk
¼ cup molasses
3 tablespoons cooking
oil

Lemon Sauce-
½ cup sugar
4 teaspoons cornstarch
Dash ground nutmeg
1 cup water
2 tablespoons butter
½ teaspoon lemon rind,
finely shredded
2 tablespoons lemon
juice

In a medium mixing bowl, stir together the flour, baking powder, cinnamon, ginger, baking soda and salt. In a large mixing bowl, beat the egg and milk, until combined. Add the molasses and cooking oil, and then beat in. Add the flour mixture to the milk mixture and stir just until blended, but still slightly lumpy.

Use about ¼ cup of the batter for each pancake, pouring onto a hot, lightly greased griddle or heavy skillet. Cook over medium heat, until browned, turning to cook the second side when the pancakes have a bubbly surface and slightly dry edges.

In a small saucepan, stir together the sugar, cornstarch and nutmeg. Stir in the water. Cook and stri, until thickened and bubbly. Cook and stir for 2 more minutes. Remove from the heat; add the butter, lemon rind and lemon juice. Stir just until the butter melts. Serve warm over the pancakes.

Orange French Toast

Beat the eggs in a large bowl. Add the orange juice, milk, vanilla, salt and orange rind and mix well. Dip the bread in the egg mixture, turning to coat all sides. Place on a baking sheet in a single layer. Pour any remaining egg mixture over the top; turn pieces a couple of times. Cover with plastic wrap and place in the refrigerator overnight.

In the morning, fry on a medium hot griddle until golden brown. Serve 3 slices per person with maple syrup. Garnish with orange slices and serve with sausage or bacon.

Yields: 6 servings
Can be stored overnight in refrigerator

6 eggs
1 cup orange juice
⅓ cup milk
¼ teaspoon vanilla extract
¼ teaspoon salt
Rind of 1 orange, finely grated
18 slices French bread, ¾-inch thick
Orange slices
Sausage or bacon

"We discovered, as so many have before us, what a jewel this lovely place is. Ouray offers much magic and this lovely hotel compliments it all beautifully."

Overnight Caramel French Toast

Temperature: 350 degrees
Cooking time: 45 minutes
Yields: 6 servings

½ **cup syrup**
½ **cup butter**
1 cup brown sugar
6 eggs
1 ½ cups milk
1 teaspoon vanilla
¼ **teaspoon salt**
12 slices bread

Melt the syrup, butter and brown sugar in a 9 x 13-inch pan. Lay 6 slices of bread over the sugar mixture. Lay the remaining 6 slices of bread on top. In a bowl, beat together the eggs, milk, vanilla and salt. Pour this mixture over the bread slices. Cover the pan and store in the refrigerator overnight.

The next morning, preheat the oven to 350 degrees. Uncover the pan and bake for 45 minutes.

Peach and Cream Cheese Oven French Toast

In a large saucepan, combine the peaches, sugar, cornstarch, water and Schnapps. Cook over medium heat, until bubbling, stirring frequently. Continue to cook 3 to 5 minutes. Remove from the heat.

Butter the bottom and sides of a 9 x 13-inch baking dish. Arrange the French bread slices bread side down in the dish. Whisk together the eggs, milk, Half & Half™ and ⅓ cup sauce from the cooked peaches. Pour half of the egg mixture over the bread slices. Allow the bread to sit for several minutes, to soak up the liquid. Using a spatula, carefully turn each slice of bread over in the dish. Pour the remaining egg mixture over the bread slices, allowing the liquid to spread evenly throughout the dish. Cut a small slit in the center of each bread slice and insert 1 cube of cream cheese. Using a slotted spoon spread the cooked peaches over the top of the bread, reserving the remaining sauce.

In a small bowl, mix together the butter, brown sugar, syrup and cinnamon. Sprinkle over the top of the bread and peaches. Bake, uncovered, in preheated 350 degree oven for 25 to 35 minutes, until the edges of the bread turn golden brown and egg mixture is cooked through. The bread should be firm, not soggy. Remove the dish from the oven and allow to stand for 5 minutes. Reheat reserved peach sauce.Arrange 2 pieces of the bread on each plate. Drizzle the sauce over each slice and serve with warm maple syrup and sausage links.

Temperature: 350 degrees
Cooking time: 25 to 35 minutes
Yields: 6 servings

3 cups fresh or frozen sliced peaches
⅔ cup sugar
1 tablespoon cornstarch
½ cup water
½ cup peach schnapps or brandy
Butter or margarine
Dry or 1 day old French bread, cut into 12, 2 to 3-inch slices
6 large eggs
½ cup milk
½ cup Half & Half™
⅓ cup sauce from cooked peaches
4 ounces cream cheese, cut into ½-inch cubes
2 tablespoons butter, softened
⅔ cup packed brown sugar
1 ½ tablespoons maple syrup
2 teaspoons cinnamon

Pear Stuffed French Toast with Sweet Orange Sauce

Temperature: medium-high
Yields: 6 servings

1 loaf French bread
3 ripe pears, peeled, cored and sliced
6 eggs
1 cup milk
1 tablespoon Grand Marnier or Amaretto
Butter for frying
Sweet Orange Sauce

Using a serrated knife, slice the French bread into 1 ½-inch thick pieces diagonally across the loaf. Starting on the crust end, slice each of the pieces down the middle, as if you were going to cut them in half, but stop ½ inch from the end. Stuff this pocket with pear slices. Beat together eggs, milk, and Grand Marnier or Amaretto.

Heat a skillet or griddle to medium high. Melt the butter in the skillet. Dip the stuffed French bread in egg batter quickly on both sides. Fry until each side is golden brown. Serve immediately, topped with the Sweet Orange Sauce.

Sweet Orange Sauce

With a serrated knife, peel oranges by first cutting a thick slice from the top and bottom, exposing the flesh. Then, cut down the sides, following the curve of the fruit and removing the whole peel, including the bitter white pith. To section orange, hold peeled fruit in one hand. With a serrated knife, slice along the membrane deep into a section. Turn the knife outward to remove section.

In a saucepan, melt butter. Stir in sugar and cook over low heat until sugar dissolves and mixture bubbles. Add orange slices and simmer 5 minutes. In a measuring cup, mix together orange juice and cornstarch. Add this to saucepan and cook until sauce thickens, stirring frequently. Serve warm over our Pear Stuffed French Toast.

Temperature: stovetop, low
Yields: 6 servings

$\frac{1}{2}$ **cup butter**
$\frac{1}{3}$ **cup sugar**
2 oranges
$\frac{1}{4}$ **cup orange juice**
$\frac{1}{4}$ **teaspoon cornstarch**

Puffed Canyon Cakes

Temperature: 475 degrees
Cooking time: 15 to 20 minutes
Yields: 1 serving

2 eggs
½ cup 2 percent milk
½ cup flour
½ teaspoon almond or vanilla extract
4 tablespoons of butter or non-stick cooking spray

Beat the eggs with a whisk or in a blender until evenly mixed. Gradually add the flour, milk and vanilla.

Melt butter or spray non-stick cooking oil in a 6-inch skillet or in 2, 4-inch ramekins. Place into oven for 15 to 20 minutes or until pancake is golden brown and very puffy.

Garnish with powdered sugar, Lexie's Raspberry-Orange syrup or fresh fruit.

"Thank you for assisting us with Meredith and Kenny's wedding reception on August 8. It was a perfect setting and very much to all of our taste. The Alps is such a beautiful Inn. We were so pleased with everything you did for us; it made our special day very relaxed and enjoyable, thank you."

Amity & Grant

Lexie's Raspberry-Orange Syrup

Heat above ingredients in pan over medium heat. Heat until well blended together. Serve warm or cold.

Serve over Puffed Canyon Cakes or over New York cheesecake.

Temperature: stovetop, medium
Cooking time: 20 minutes
Yields: 4 servings

1 bag frozen raspberries
2 cups orange marmalade

"Thank you for your hospitality. I enjoyed my stay at the Alps & will recommend it highly. I love the lodge-like ambience & the big tub in the Goldhill room."

Nancy

Rocky Mountain Blueberry French Toast

Temperature: 350 degrees
Cooking time: 40 minutes
Yields: 8 servings

12 slices stale French bread cut into 1-inch cubes
16 ounces cream cheese, chilled and cut into 1-inch cubes
1 cup fresh blueberries, rinsed and drained
12 large eggs
⅓ cup maple syrup
2 cups milk

Generously grease 8 au gratin dishes. Place half of the bread cubes in the dishes. Scatter the cream cheese over the bread and sprinkle with 1 cup of the berries. Arrange the remaining bread cubes over the berries. In a large bowl combine the eggs, syrup and milk. Mix and pour evenly over the bread-cheese mixture. Spray the undersides of 8 pieces of foil generously with a non-stick vegetable spray and cover each au gratin dish. Refrigerate overnight.

In the morning, set the dishes out to bring them to room temperature. Bake in a 350 degree oven, covered, for 25 minutes. Uncover and bake an additional 15 minutes or until puffed and golden. Serve with blueberry syrup.

"Nothing short of Heaven!! We've never been so relaxed nor felt so comfortable. The food is absolutely 4 stars."

Amy and Jason

Blueberry Syrup

Combine the sugar, cornstarch and water over medium-high heat. Cook for 5 minutes or until thickened. Stir occasionally. Stir in the blueberries and simmer for 10 minutes or until the blueberries burst. Add the butter. Stir until melted. Drizzle over French toast.

Temperature: stovetop, medium-high
Cooking time: 5 minutes
Yields: 8 servings

1 cup sugar
2 tablespoons cornstarch
1 cup water
1 cup fresh blueberries, rinsed and drained
1 tablespoon unsalted butter

"Cattail Creek has it all. It's in a league with the very elite. The floor plan, the quality furnishings, the great breakfasts to start the day, the friendly home like setting, and above all, your caring and concern for guests and their happiness is a joy to behold."

Marie and Ed
Vermont

Appetizers

Black Olive Pesto

Combine all the ingredients in a food processor, pulsing until the mixture has the consistency of pesto. If no food processor is available, simply chop by hand.

Note: If desired, an Anchovy may be added

$\frac{1}{2}$ cup Kalamata olives
$\frac{1}{4}$ cup black olives
$\frac{1}{2}$ lemon, zested and
  juiced
1 teaspoon garlic,
  minced
2 teaspoons olive oil
2 teaspoons capers,
  drained
Salt and pepper to taste

"Great People, great food, great place."

Mona & Paul
Grant, MN

Dreamy Cheese Nut Roll

Yields: 12 servings

1, 8-ounce package cream cheese
½ cup bleu cheese, crumbled
1 teaspoon lemon juice
½ teaspoon salt
Salted peanuts, chopped
Dash of Worcestershire sauce
3 tablespoons green onion, finely chopped
¼ teaspoon garlic salt
A little cream, if needed

Mix all ingredients, except for the peanuts. Form into the shape or shapes of your choice. Roll it in the chopped and salted peanuts. Chill in the refrigerator. Decorate with parsley or flowers just prior to serving.

German Cheese Log

Put all the ingredients, except for the chili pepper, in a food processor. Process until just blended. Roll into a 2-inch log. Roll the log in the chili pepper to coat. Wrap the coated log in wax paper.

Garnish with parsley or leaf lettuce. Slice and serve with snack crackers of your choice.

Temperature: 40 degrees
Yields: 15 to 20 servings
Can be stored for up to 2
  months in the refrigerator

$1/2$ **pound medium**
  Cheddar cheese
8 ounces cream cheese
$1/2$ **teaspoon garlic salt**
1 cup pecans
Ground chili pepper or
  chili seasoning

Herbed Cheese Spread

Yields: 2 Cups
Can be stored for 1 week
in refrigerator

32 ounces cream cheese
2 scallions, minced
2 large garlic cloves,
minced
1 teaspoon lemon juice
1 teaspoon basil
1 teaspoon marjoram
1 teaspoon thyme
1 teaspoon Beau Monde
½ teaspoon tarragon
½ teaspoon dill
Dash of salt
Dash of cayenne pepper
Assorted crackers

Bring cream cheese to room temperature. Blend in all other ingredients with the exception of the crackers. Serve with assorted crackers.

"We have had a wonderful time together at the St. Elmo. The skiing was fun, the food tasty and the company superb."

Jackie's Crab Dip

Soften the cream cheese and mix with the sour cream. Shred the crabmeat and mix with all the other ingredients. Spread evenly over the bottom of a quiche pan. Sprinkle Parmesan cheese over top and bake in a 350 degree oven for 10 to 15 minutes. Serve hot with stone wheat thins or crackers of your choice.

Temperature: 350 degrees
Cooking time: 10 to 15
  minutes
Yields: 20 servings
Can refrigerate overnight
  and bake the next day

  1 pound crab or
    imitation crab
  8 ounces cream cheese
  1 cup sour cream
  1 tablespoon cocktail
    sauce
  $\frac{1}{2}$ cup onion, chopped
  $\frac{1}{2}$ cup Parmesan cheese
  Pepper to taste

Mushroom Canapes

Temperature: 400 degrees
Cooking time: 10 to 12
  minutes
Yields: 24 servings

2 pie shells, unbaked
½ pound mushrooms,
  sliced
1 medium onion,
  chopped
3 tablespoons butter
2 tablespoons flour
¼ cup sour cream
¼ teaspoon thyme
¼ teaspoon pepper
¼ teaspoon salt
1 tablespoon sherry

Sauté the mushrooms and onion in butter in a large frying pan, until the onions are cooked through. Add the flour and spices. Stir well and remove from heat. Add the sour cream and sherry and mix together well. Set aside. Roll a pie shell out on a floured surface to ⅛-inch thickness. Use a small round cookie cutter or other similarly sized utensil to cut the pastry into 2-inch rounds. Place the rounds in a greased mini-muffin pan. Fill each pocket with the mushroom mixture. Bake at 400 degrees in preheated oven for 10 to 12 minutes.

These canapes can be frozen after baking and stored 6 to 8 weeks. To reheat, place the frozen canapes on a cookie sheet and place in a 350 degree oven for 20 minutes.

"Our breakfast was a gourmet experience, so much of an assortment for every varied appetite (my husband enjoys the specials and I prefer a lighter fare)."

Parmesan Chicken Wings

Prepare the seasoning mix in a bowl. Melt the butter and pour into a separate bowl. Dip the chicken wings in the butter, then roll in the seasoning mix. Place the wings on a foil covered cookie sheet. Bake at 350 degrees for 30 to 45 minutes. If using boneless chicken breasts in place of the wings, reduce the cooking time to 30 minutes.

"Thank you for your kindness and hospitality. I look forward to bringing an event here soon! I felt like 'Queen Anne' in the Goldhill room. I truly enjoyed my stay and will be back."

Temperature: 350 degrees
Cooking time: 30 to 45 minutes

4 pounds chicken wings, separated, wing tips removed
1 cup butter

Seasoning Mix-
1 $\frac{1}{2}$ cups Parmesan cheese, grated
4 tablespoons parsley, fresh, chopped
4 tablespoons paprika
3 tablespoons oregano
2 teaspoons black pepper
1 teaspoon white pepper

Pizza Dip

Temperature: 350 degrees
Cooking time: 15 minutes
Yields: 10 servings

8 ounces cream cheese
8 ounces sour cream
1 onion, chopped
1 jar spaghetti sauce
Pepperoni
8 ounces mozzarella
** cheese**
Thick crackers or nacho
** chips**

Preheat oven to 350 degrees. Mix the cream cheese, sour cream and chopped onion. Spread in a round glass quiche pan or 10-inch pie pan. Spread the spaghetti sauce and top with pepperoni. Bake for 10 minutes. Top with the mozzarella cheese. Bake 5 minutes more.

Serve with thick crackers or nacho chips.

"It was really difficult to come back to civilization after spending a wonderful week at Elk Mountain Ranch. We were really relaxed and enjoyed every minute of our week—even the hailstorm. This was the first vacation that Paul and I truly wanted to extend another week. Leaving for home was rather sad, like leaving our family behind. Usually on a vacation there is something that can be improved, but we could find nothing that could be made better. Excellent food, super staff, and so much to do. We do plan to return."

Paul and Elaine
Liverpool, NY

Red Pepper Cheese Spread

Bring cream cheese to room temperature. Cut the red pepper in half lengthwise and remove the stem and seeds. Chop red pepper and olives by hand or in food processor. Blend all ingredients except the crackers. Serve with assorted crackers.

Yields: 3 ½ cups
Can be stored for 1 week
** in refrigerator**

32 ounces cream cheese
1 red bell pepper
2 handfuls olives
¾ cup onion, chopped
¾ cup sour cream
Assorted crackers

Salmon Mousse

Temperature: stovetop, boiling
Can be stored for 1 week in the refrigerator

2 envelopes unflavored gelatin
½ cup cold water
1 cup boiling water
1 tablespoon vinegar
3 tablespoons lemon juice
1 cup mayonnaise
1 cup heavy cream, firmly whipped
½ teaspoon salt
1 tablespoon Worcestershire sauce
2 cups cucumber or celery, finely chopped
1 medium size onion, grated
1, 1-pound can salmon

Soak the gelatin in cold water, then dissolve in boiling water. Add the vinegar and lemon juice and place in the refrigerator to thicken. Flake the salmon and combine with the mayonnaise and whipped cream. Add to the other ingredients. Pour into oiled 6-cup mold and chill until firm, preferably overnight.

Serve on a chilled platter with large crackers.

Sara's Stuffed Mushrooms

Chop the crab and shrimp and mix together. Sauté the mix with butter and garlic for 2 to 3 minutes. Add the crackers and onions. Mix should have a slightly tacky, dry stuffing consistency. Add more butter, if necessary. Remove the stems from the mushrooms and fill the caps with the mixture.

Place in a covered frying pan on low heat and top with cheese. Alternatively, you can bake the mushrooms in a 350 degree oven. In any case, cook until the cheese is melted or the mushrooms are warm, but slightly firm. Do not over cook. Serve warm.

Temperature: 350 degrees
Yields: 30 to 50 mushrooms

2 pounds large mushrooms
1 package salad shrimp
1 pound package of crabmeat
4 cups crushed Ritz crackers
1 ½ teaspoons garlic, minced
¼ cup green onions, chopped
1 stick butter, melted
½ pound grated Mozzarella cheese

"What pure delight it has been staying here again. Part of our love for Vail is your friendship, hospitality and the warmth of new friends we have met here. Thanks always."

Sheep Dip

Yields: 3 cups

**12 artichoke bottoms,
  sliced
¾ pound cream cheese
½ cup heavy whipping
  cream
1 tablespoon garlic,
  chopped
¼ pound fresh spinach,
  chopped
¼ pound sour cream
⅛ pound Parmesan
  cheese**

Mix together all of the ingredients. Heat in a saucepan, stirring frequently.

Serve with warm Pita chips or bagels

Smoked Trout Mousse

Mix all ingredients in medium bowl. Add salt and pepper to taste. Serve at room temperature. Serve as an elegant appetizer accompanied by crackers or toasted bread.

Yields: 8 servings

1 cup Ricotta cheese
1 cup smoked trout, chopped
2 tablespoons prepared horseradish
2 tablespoons scallion, chopped
2 tablespoons fresh dill, chopped
2 teaspoons lemon juice

Salads & Dressings

Aunt Eleanor's Shrimp Salad

Yields: 4 servings

- 1 pound macaroni rings
- 1 medium onion, diced
- 2 stalks celery, diced
- 1 teaspoon crushed parsley
- Pepper and garlic salt, to taste
- 1 cup mayonnaise
- 1 teaspoon Dijon mustard
- 1 teaspoon sugar
- 1 pound cooked mini shrimp

Boil pasta just until tender, then drain. Rinse in cold water and add onion, celery, parsley, pepper and garlic salt. Refrigerate overnight. Combine the mayonnaise, mustard, sugar and shrimp. Add the two mixtures together a couple of hours before serving. Can substitute crab or lobster in place of shrimp.

Caesar Salad Dressing

Yields: 50 servings

7 ½ ounces canned
  anchovy fillets
⅓ cup garlic cloves
1 ½ cups pasteurized
  egg substitute
1 ¾ cups lemon juice
  (about 7 lemons)
1 tablespoon plus ½
  teaspoon dry mustard
1 ¾ cups plain non-fat
  yogurt
7 tablespoons
  Worcestershire sauce
7 tablespoons wine
  vinegar
1 ⅓ cups olive oil
1 teaspoon Tabasco™
  sauce
1 ¼ cups grated
  Parmesan cheese

Mix the anchovy filets, Worcestershire sauce, garlic, wine vinegar, egg substitute, olive oil, lemon juice, dry mustard and Tabasco™ sauce in a blender until nearly smooth. Stir in the grated Parmesan cheese and yogurt.

Serve over Romaine lettuce with additional Parmesan cheese and garlic.

Coca Cola Salad

Drain the cherries and pineapple into a saucepan and heat the juices to a boil. Add the gelatins, stirring until dissolved. Add the cola, cherries, pineapple and nuts. Pour into a Jello mold and refrigerate until set. Unmold onto lettuce, and then grate the frozen cream cheese over the top to give the appearance of snow.

1 can seedless white cherries
1 large can crushed pineapple
1 package raspberry gelatin
1 package cherry gelatin
2 cans Coca Cola™
1 cup pecans
8 ounces cream cheese, frozen

"Our stay at the Inn on Valentine's Day was so wonderful! Our room was charming, the food delicious and the staff friendly & Helpful. And the fireplaces were warm & interesting too! Shane and I will definitely be back."

Stormy

Colorado Pine Nut Salad

Yields: 6 servings

¼ cup pine nuts
2 cloves garlic
1 cup water
¼ teaspoon salt
1 teaspoon Dijon
  mustard
2 tablespoons white wine
  vinegar
½ cup virgin olive oil
1 large head romaine
  lettuce, torn into pieces
Freshly ground black
pepper to taste
¼ cup Parmesan
  cheese, coarsely
  shredded

Toast the pine nuts under the broiler, until golden brown. Watch them carefully! Set aside.

In a small saucepan, boil the garlic in water for 10 minutes; drain. In a large salad bowl, mash the garlic and salt to a paste. Whisk in the mustard and vinegar. Add the oil in a stream, whisking the dressing until the oil is emulsified. Add the romaine; toss well and season with the pepper. Sprinkle the Parmesan and pine nuts over the salad and serve.

For a festive salad, try garnishing with a few cranberries.

Curried Turkey Salad

In a medium stainless steel bowl, mix the mayonnaise, curry powder and dill weed until smooth. Add diced apples and diced turkey meat and mix until completely coated. In a microwave-safe bowl mix lemon juice and raisins; cover and microwave on high setting for 30 seconds. Add raisins to the apples and turkey; mix well. Serve on a bed of shaved carrots and place pepper rings on top.

Serve with fresh hot French bread.

"Wonderful place to build sweet memories."

Yields: 4 servings
Can be stored for 4 to 5
  days refrigerated

$\frac{1}{3}$ **cup mayonnaise**
3 tablespoons curry
  powder
1 teaspoon dried dill
  weed
1 $\frac{1}{2}$ cups cooked turkey
  meat, diced
3 green apples, peeled,
  cored and diced
2 teaspoons lemon juice
1 cup raisins
2 large carrots, shaved
10 mild pickled pepper
  rings for garnish

Mandarin Salad

Temperature: stovetop,
  medium
Cooking time: 10 minutes
Yields: 4 to 6 servings

Salad-
  1/4 cup cashews
  1 tablespoon plus 1
    teaspoon sugar
  1 cup chopped celery
    with leaves
  2 green onions with tops,
    thinly sliced
  1/4 head lettuce, torn
  1/4 bunch romaine
    lettuce or spinach, torn
  11 ounces mandarin
    oranges

Dressing-
  1/4 cup vegetable oil
  2 tablespoons sugar
  2 tablespoons white
    vinegar
  1 tablespoon snipped
    parsley
  1/4 teaspoon salt
  Dash pepper and red
    pepper sauce

Combine ingredients for the dressing in a blender. Mix and chill.

Cook the cashews and sugar over medium heat, stirring constantly until sugar is melted and nuts are browned (approximately 10 minutes). Cool and break apart.

Combine lettuce, celery and onions. Arrange on salad plates. Place 4 or more orange slices on top and sprinkle salads with caramelized cashews. Drizzle 1 tablespoon of dressing on each salad.

"We'll be back! The meals were excellent-loved the variety & the service with a smile! Made every meal that much more enjoyable."

Oven Roasted Tomato Relish

Start with the oven roasted tomatoes. Preheat the oven to 250 degrees. In a large mixing bowl combine all ingredients. Toss well and let sit 15 minutes. Line a cookie sheet with a large wire rack (cake rack, used for cooling). Spread tomatoes in a single layer on rack (reserve the juice for the relish). Place in oven for approximately 1 hour or until they look fairly dry but not crispy. Remove and let cool.

To make the relish, combine the oven-roasted tomatoes with the relish ingredients and the reserved juice; mix well. Cover and refrigerate at least 3 hours to allow the flavors to marry.

Temperature: 250 degrees
Cooking time: 1 hour
Yields: 1 cup

Oven Roasted Tomatoes-
  1 ½ pounds Roma tomatoes, cored and sliced ¼-inch thick
  4 tablespoons Olive oil
  1 ½ tablespoons dried basil
  1 ½ tablespoons dried oregano
  1 tablespoon garlic, minced
  1 tablespoon granulated garlic
  1 tablespoon Kosher salt
  Fresh ground pepper

Relish Ingredients-
  ⅛ cup parsley, chopped
  ¼ cup red onion, minced
  1 tablespoon Sherry wine vinegar
  1 tablespoon Olive oil
  1 tablespoon fresh basil, chopped
  ½ tablespoon fresh oregano, chopped
  Salt and pepper to taste

Peppery Nasturtium Salmon Salad

Yields: 4 servings

**4 cups packed greens
(include spinach, ice-
berg & leaf lettuce)
1 can pink Alaskan
Salmon
3 tablespoons olive oil
½ cup chopped onion
6 tablespoons Nasturtium
vinegar or red wine
vinegar
2 tablespoons water
1 teaspoon sugar
2 teaspoons dried,
crushed red chilies
1 tablespoon olive oil
2 teaspoons Dijon
mustard
Salt and pepper to taste
12 to 14 fresh Nasturtium
blossoms
Fresh basil sprigs for
garnish**

Place the greens in large bowl and chill. Heat the olive oil in a skillet over medium heat. Add the chopped onions and sauté until translucent. Add the vinegar, water, sugar and chilies and bring to a boil. Remove from the heat and let cool. Mix the olive oil and mustard into a paste. Add the salt and pepper to taste. Add the Salmon chunks and stir carefully; chill.

To serve, toss the salmon mixture with the salad greens. Garnish with the Nasturtium blossoms and basil sprigs.

Variation: Substitute 1 pound of Italian sausage for the salmon.

"Enjoyed my return to Castle Marne & my time in the garden, relaxing among the spring flowers—oops-summer already. Sorry I had to miss breakfast—see you in September I hope. Thanks for the great visit Diane and Jim."

*Shari
Huntington Beach, CA*

Taco Salad

Mix the enchilada and tomato sauces with the sugar in a saucepan over medium heat. In a separate pan, mix the kidney beans and butter together over medium heat. In a fry pan, brown the ground beef.

In an 11 x 13-inch pan, layer in the ingredients in the following order: Nacho chips, browned ground beef, half the cheese, bean/butter mixture, chopped vegetables and olives. Just before serving pour the hot sauce mixture over the top. Sprinkle the remaining cheese over the top.

Yields: 8 to 10 servings

2 pounds ground beef
12 ounces nacho chips
**1 medium head of
lettuce, chopped**
2 tomatoes, chopped
1 green pepper, chopped
**1 medium onion,
chopped**
1 can sliced black olives
**1 medium can kidney
beans**
1 tablespoon butter
**10 ounces enchilada
sauce**
15 ounces tomato sauce
$\frac{1}{8}$ teaspoon sugar
2 to 3 cups grated cheese

Tomato, Garlic, Artichoke and Kalamata Vinaigrette

Yields: 2 cups

4 Roma tomatoes,
  peeled, seeded and
  diced
1 shallot, minced
3 cloves garlic, minced
$1/4$ cup red wine vinegar
$1/2$ cup V-8™ juice
1 cup Olive oil
1, 6-ounce can artichoke
  hearts in olive oil,
  drained, quartered, oil
  reserved
$1/4$ cup Kalamata olives,
  julienned
Kosher salt and fresh
  ground black pepper to
  taste

Core the tops of the tomatoes and cut an "X" in the bottom. Drop into a pot of boiling water for about 15 to 20 seconds. The time will vary depending on ripeness of tomatoes. Remove from the water and drop into an ice bath to stop the cooking. Using a paring knife carefully peel the tomatoes, quarter and seed. Dice into $1/4$-inch chunks.

Drain the artichoke hearts, quarter and set aside. Place the shallot, garlic, vinegar and V-8 juice in a bowl. Slowly whisk in the olive oil and the reserved olive oil from the artichokes. Fold in the diced tomatoes, artichoke hearts, and olives. Season to taste with the salt and pepper. Let this vinaigrette sit for at least 3 hours before use to allow the flavors to marry.

Warm Goat Cheese Salad

To start the dressing, heat the olive oil and crisp the Panchetta in a pan. Turn off the stove and add the thyme, butter, sherry, vinegar, roasted red pepper, salt and pepper to the pan. When the pan has cooled some, add in the goat cheese and mix well.

Put the mixed greens into a bowl and cover them with the warm dressing.

Cooking time: 15 minutes
Yields: 1 serving

1 cup mixed greens

Dressing-
1 ounce Panchetta
$\frac{1}{2}$ ounce goat cheese
Salt to taste
Pepper to taste
$\frac{1}{2}$ red pepper
1 $\frac{1}{2}$ ounces sherry
   vinegar
$\frac{1}{2}$ ounce butter
1 ounce olive oil
$\frac{1}{4}$ teaspoon thyme

Soups & Stews

Carrot Ginger Soup

Sauté the onion, garlic and ginger in unsalted butter. Add the curry, stock, wine and carrots. Let simmer for 30 to 45 minutes, covered. When slightly cooled, puree the soup. Add lemon juice; season with salt and pepper. Garnish with chopped parsley.

Temperature: stovetop, simmer
Yields: 8 servings

6 tablespoons unsalted butter
1 large yellow onion
¼ cup ginger, minced
3 cloves garlic, minced
Pinch of curry
Parsley for garnish
7 cups chicken stock
1 cup dry, white wine
1 ½ pounds carrots
2 tablespoons lemon juice
Salt and pepper to taste

Cheesy Potato Soup

Temperature: stovetop, medium
Yields: 4 servings

1 cup carrots, chopped
½ cup celery, chopped
½ cup onion, chopped
½ cup hot water
1 chicken bouillon cube
¼ teaspoon salt
⅛ teaspoon pepper
1 ½ cups milk
1 cup Cheddar cheese, shredded
1 tablespoon fresh parsley, chopped
2 cups potatoes, cubed

In a 2-quart saucepan, combine the potatoes, carrots, celery, onion, water, bouillon, salt and pepper. Cover and cook until the vegetables are tender. Blend in a food processor until coarsely pureed. Return to the saucepan. Blend in the milk and cheese. Cover and cook until the cheese melts. Garnish with fresh, chopped parsley.

Drunken Mushroom Soup

Sauté the white onion, red onion, scallions and garlic in butter. Add the sherry, white wine, chicken base and water. Simmer for 30 minutes. Add the marjoram, sweet ground basil and pepper. Puree the mushrooms and add to the mixture. Simmer for another 20 to 30 minutes. Mixture should be thick in that there are LOTS of mushroom bits and very little broth.

Cooking time: 50 to 60 minutes
Yields: 10 to 20 servings

1 tablespoon butter
1 white onion, pureed
1 red onion, pureed
½ cup scallions (green onions)
1 tablespoon garlic
2 cups sherry
6 cups white wine
10 cups chicken base and water
1 tablespoon marjoram
1 tablespoon sweet ground basil
Pepper to taste
8 to 10 cups mushrooms

"Few vacation spots leave one with an emotional attachment that results in a sincere sadness when it's time to leave"

Bill

Hall of Fame Jambalaya

**Temperature: stovetop,
  medium-high
Cooking time: 20 minutes
Yields: 6 servings
Can be stored for 5 days in
  refrigerator or frozen.**

**½ cup onion, diced
1 ½ cups tomato, diced
½ cup celery, diced
2 tablespoons Creole
  seasoning
1 tablespoon pepper
1 tablespoon salt
1 cup red peppers, diced
1 cup yellow peppers,
  diced
½ cup green peppers,
  diced
1 cup tomato paste
2 cups white wine to
  deglaze pans**

Preheat 2 sauté pans on medium high heat. Sauté all garden vegetables to an Aldente texture. Cook the tomatoes until broken down to a stewed base. Fold all the ingredients, including spices, into the stewed base. Simmer for approximately 7 ½ minutes. Serve over Rissotto. Garnish with fresh Mexican Cilantro sprigs

Italian Sausage Soup with Tortellini

Brown the sausage; drain. Mix with the rest of the ingredients, excepting the tortellini and peas, in a 4 or 5-quart soup pot. Bring to a slow boil and cook for 30 minutes or until the carrots are done. Add the tortellini according to cooking time on package, depending on whether they are frozen or dry. Add the frozen peas 5 minutes before the soup is done, allowing just long enough for them to thaw. Serve with crusty bread and a sprinkle of Parmesan cheese on top.

"Thanks for a wonderful week! We appreciate all your kindness, patience and for making us feel so at home during our stay at your beautiful ranch!"

Temperature: stovetop, boiling,
Cooking time: 45 minutes
Yields: 8 to 10 servings

1 pound Italian sausage
2 cloves garlic, minced
3 leeks, diced
2 quarts water
2 carrots, diced
1 celery heart, diced
2, 15-ounce cans crushed tomatoes
Pinch of oregano, basil and pepper
2 tablespoons concentrated chicken soup base
1, 12-ounce package frozen or dried tortellini
1, 10-ounce box frozen peas

SAN JUAN GUEST RANCH

Ranch Chili

Temperature: stovetop,
  medium
Cooking time: 2 hours
Yields: 15 to 20 servings
Can be frozen and stored
  for up to 4 weeks

5 pounds stew meat, cut
  into bite size pieces
1, #10 can diced
  tomatoes
1, #10 can kidney beans
2 small cans tomato
  paste
$\frac{1}{2}$ cup beef base
1 onion, chopped
2 tablespoons oil
$\frac{1}{4}$ cup cumin
4 tablespoons garlic
  powder
$\frac{1}{2}$ cup chili powder or
  to taste

In a large pot, brown the stew meat with the oil and onion. Add the diced tomatoes, tomato paste, beef base and spices. Simmer for 1 hour. Add the kidney beans and simmer for an additional hour.

Serve with grated Cheddar cheese and sour cream. Add a baked potato and salad for a hearty winter lunch.

Smoked Corn and Shrimp Chowder

In a small saucepan cover the potatoes with water and cook until tender, but not mushy; drain and set aside. In a large pot sauté the bacon, onions and garlic until translucent, about 10 minutes. Stir in the flour to thicken slightly. Add the milk and corn, and then heat through. Add the potatoes. Season with the smoke favoring and pepper. Adjust salt if necessary and add the shrimp. Prior to serving add the heavy cream and heat through. Garnish with chopped fresh parsley, if desired.

Temperature: stovetop, medium
Cooking time: 20 minutes
Yields: 4 to 6 servings

3 cups water
3 cups potatoes, scrubbed, diced to 1-inch cubes
2 ounces bacon, cut in ½-inch pieces
2 cups onions, finely chopped
½ tablespoon garlic, minced
3 tablespoons flour
1 ½ cups yellow corn kernels
2 cups baby shrimp, cooked
1 ½ teaspoons smoke flavoring
1 teaspoon white pepper, ground
2 quarts milk
1 pint heavy cream

Tortellini Soup

Cooking time: 2 to 3
 hours
Yields: 10 servings

12 ¾ ounces Italian
 sausage
¾ clove chopped garlic
⅓ medium onion,
 chopped
2 ⅓ cups beef broth
⅓ cup water
1 ⅔ cups fresh
 tomatoes, chopped and
 peeled
1 ⅔ cups tomato sauce
1 large carrot, peeled
 and chopped
¾ tablespoon oregano
¾ teaspoon basil, dried
¾ tablespoon parsley,
 dried
⅔ bay leaf
⅓ zucchini, chopped
3 or 4, 10-ounce
 packages fresh or
 frozen tortellini, cheese
 filled only
1 package of spinach
 pasta for color

Brown the sausage, keeping it in large chunks. Remove the browned meat from the pan, reserving 8 tablespoons of the oil. Sauté the onion and garlic in the reserved drippings. In a large soup pot, mix all the ingredients, with the exception of the zucchini and tortellini. Add the sausage. Bring to a boil and then lower the heat. Simmer the soup for 2 to 3 hours. Approximately 45 minutes before serving, add the tortellini and zucchini; simmer until the tortellini are done.

Garnish with fresh grated Parmesan cheese.

White Chili

Brown the ground turkey. Add the onion, chilies, bouillon, chili powder and water. Simmer for 10 minutes. Add the beans and a little more water, if necessary. Simmer for an additional 30 minutes. Top with a shredded cheese, such as Monterey Jack or Cheddar, if desired.

Temperature: stovetop, simmer
Cooking time: 40 minutes

1 pound ground turkey
1 medium onion, chopped
4 ounce can diced green chilies
2 teaspoons chicken bouillon granules
1 teaspoon chili powder
1 cup water
3, 15-ounce cans Great Northern™ beans

Y2K Soup For You and The Neighbors

Temperature: medium-high
Cooking time: 20 minutes
Yields: 8 to 12 servings
Can be stored for several days refrigerated

Soup-
2, 15-ounce cans extra sweet whole kernel corn
2, 15-ounce cans Southwestern black beans
2, 14 ½-ounce cans Mexican style stewed tomatoes
1, 4-ounce can chopped green chilies
2 cans of water (use 15 ounce can)

Tasty Additions-
3 to 4 chicken breasts, boned and skinned
¼ cup cilantro, chopped
Sharp Cheddar cheese, shredded
Tortilla chips or tortillas

Cook the chicken breasts on the grill before you combine the canned food items. Season well with garlic salt. Let cool. When cool to the touch, tear chicken into bite size pieces.

Place all the canned ingredients in a large pot and cook on the grill (either propane or charcoal works fine when there is no electricity) until it boils. Add the cooked chicken pieces.

Add cilantro 5 to 10 minutes before serving. When ready to serve, ladle into bowls and sprinkle about ¼ cup cheese into each bowl. Serve with tortillas or crumbled chips on top of the cheese.

Garnish with fresh cilantro leaves. Soup is always good with salad and sandwich.

This recipe was given to guests before the new millennium to help them prepare for the Y2K "bugs" that didn't occur as it turns out. The recipe was first tried on guests at the Abriendo Inn when there was no electricity during the infamous October 1997 snowstorm. There was a house full of guests that couldn't go anywhere and we had to serve more than just breakfast.

Abriendo Inn
300 West Abriendo Ave.
Pueblo, CO 81004
719-544-2703
Fax: 719-542-6544
Email: abriendo@rmi.net
Web: www.bedandbreakfastinns.org/abriendo
Kerrelyn McCafferty Trent, Innkeeper

From the spiral staircase to the curved stained glass windows and parquet floors, you know that you are entering a special place. Feel like you belong at the inn and absorb the tranquility while strolling the park-like grounds or walking through the tree-lined neighborhoods and the nearby historic Union Avenue. Many restaurants, shops, galleries, and other attractions are all within five minutes of the inn. Rare architectural features, elegant rooms, and full gourmet breakfasts refresh the guests at this historic estate home in the heart of Pueblo.

Allaire Timbers Inn
9511 Hwy 9-South Main
PO Box 4653
Breckenridge, CO 80424
970-453-7530
Fax: 970-453-8699
Toll Free: 800-624-4904 (except Colorado)
Email: allairetimbers@worldnet.att.net
Web: www.allairetimbers.com
Jack and Kathy Gumph, Innkeepers

A contemporary ten-room log inn offering private baths, hot tubs, fireplaces and spectacular mountain views. Tucked into the trees at the south end of historic Main Street, the award-winning Allaire Timbers Inn opened its doors to guests in 1991. The log cabin construction features native Colorado lodgepole pine, its faint outdoorsy aroma ever-present. Hearty breakfasts, afternoon refreshments, a relaxing outdoor hot tub and personalized hospitality make the Allaire Timbers Inn the perfect romantic getaway.

**Alpine Mountain Ranch
PO Box 248
Allenspark, CO 80510
303-747-2532
Toll Free: 800-578-3598
Email: info@alpinemountainranch.com
Web: www.alpinemountainranch.com**

Backing up to Roosevelt National Forrest and Rocky Mountain National Park, guests of the ranch can ride and hike through pristine alpine forests, streams and lakes. They offer the informal charm of a Western/Colorado dude ranch, with optional excursions to an authentic homestead cattle ranch only 15 miles and 100 years away. Activities include: an extensive horse program, pack/fishing trips, wagon rides, overnight excursions, cookouts, a children's program, swimming and soaking in their heated pool and unique outdoor hot tub. Home style cooking, friendly staff, comfortable accommodations and breathtaking views will have you coming back for more.

**The Alps Boulder Canyon Inn
38619 Boulder Canyon Drive
Boulder, CO 80302
303-444-5445
Fax: 303-444-5522
Toll Free: 800-414-2577
Email: alpsinn@aol.com
Web: www.alpsinn.com
Vanderhart and Ruzicka Families, Innkeepers**

Come visit Boulder's most award winning inn, the Alps Boulder Canyon Inn named "Best of Westword" magazine and "Top of the Town" in Colorado's 5280 magazine. Only 5 minutes from the heart of downtown Boulder, yet nestled among the pines in Boulder Canyon, the Alps offers visitors to Boulder luxurious accommodations as well as knowledgeable and attentive service. Within minutes of the inn are the University of Colorado, Boulder's Pearl Street Pedestrian Mall, downtown shops, restaurants, award winning library and museums.

Aspen Canyon Ranch
13206 County Road #3, Star Route
Parshall, CO 80468
970-725-3600
Toll Free: 800-321-1357
Email: acr@imageline.com
Web: www.aspencanyon.com
The Roderick Family

Guests stay in log cabins named Deer, Elk and Trout Lodge. Each is located along the Williams Fork River with porches, log furniture, natural gas rock fireplaces, carpeting, refrigerators, coffee makers and old-fashioned swings. You will find a jar of freshly baked cookies in your room each day. The main lodge houses the dining room and living rooms with two cozy fireplaces and a big wonderful porch. Aspen Canyon Ranch is committed to food excellence on your behalf and we are certain you will look forward to each meal. From breakfast to dinner our meals are homemade and delicious. Special diets can be accommodated with advance notice. Wine and liquor can also be picked up with advance notice.

Bar Lazy J Guest Ranch
Box ND
Parshall, CO 80468
970-725-3437
Fax: 970-725-0121
Toll Free: 800-396-6279
Email: BarLazyJ@rkymtnhi.com
Web: www.barlazyj.com
Jerry & Cheri Helmicki

Bar Lazy J is nestled in a peaceful valley along the banks of the Colorado River. Opened in 1912, Bar Lazy J is considered the oldest continuously operating guest ranch in the state. The ranch has a fascinating history. While the original log lodge and cabins have been modernized, everything possible has been done to retain the look and atmosphere of the 'Old West'. You will enjoy stepping into the past.

The Black Bear Inn
2405 Elliott Road
Vail, CO 81657
970-476-1304
Fax: 970-476-0433
Web: www.vail.net/blackbear and
www.bedandbreakfastinns.org/blackbear
David and Jessie Edeen, Innkeepers

The Black Bear Inn of Vail is everything you would expect to find in a Rocky Mountain get-away. Located along the banks of Gore Creek on its own secluded site, it is close to the slopes and other amenities to make your stay convenient and enjoyable. The handcrafted log cabin has 12 guest rooms, each with its own tiled bath, queen or twin bed with down comforter and sitting area to relax in any time of day. Enjoy the great room with the warmth of the antique stove and newfound friends or enjoy our new game room with pool table, pinball and card table for that competitive spirit. The inn also has an executive conference room (for 12) to handle your business needs. Full breakfast, afternoon appetizers included.

The Briar Rose
2151 Arapahoe Avenue
Boulder, CO 80302
303-442-3007
Fax: 303-786-8440
Email: brbbx@aol.com
Web: www.globalmall.com/brose
Margaret & Bob Weisenbach,
Innkeepers

Travel to the Briar Rose Bed and Breakfast for the ultimate accommodations in Boulder, Colorado in the beautiful Rocky Mountains. Enjoy skiing, hiking, and biking during your vacation at this romantic inn near the University of Colorado. Also, you can schedule your wedding reception or small meetings with lodging at this Victorian bed and breakfast.

C Lazy U Ranch
PO Box 379
Granby, CO 80446
970-887-3344
Email: Ranch@CLazyu.com
Web: www.CLazyu.com
The Clark Murray Family

Since 1946, the C Lazy U Ranch has been treating guests to the very finest in gracious Western hospitality. It's earned them both the prestigious Mobil Travel Guide "Five Star" Award and the American Automobile Association "Five Diamond" Award–year after year. It's also earned them the loyalty of guests worldwide that return to the C Lazy U to vacation season after season. At C Lazy U Ranch, there's still plenty of room to stretch out. Time to relax; range to ride; mountains to explore; fish to catch. All the simple pleasures to experience.

Castle Marne
1572 Race Street
Denver, CO 80206
303-331-0621
Fax: 303-331-0623
Toll Free: 800-926-2763
Email: info@castlemarne.com
Web: www.castlemarne.com
The Peiker Family, Innkeepers

Fall under the spell of one of Denver's grandest historic mansions. Built in 1889, Castle Marne is listed on the National Register of Historic Structures, and located in the Wyman Historic District. A stay at Castle Marne combines Old World elegance and Victorian charm with modern-day convenience and comfort. Each room is a unique experience in pampered luxury. Carefully chosen furnishings bring together authentic period antiques, family heirlooms, and exacting reproductions to create the mood of long-ago charm and romance.

Cattail Creek Inn
2665 Abarr Drive
Loveland, CO 80538
970-667-7600
Fax: 970-667-8968
Toll Free: 800-572-2466
Email: ccinn@oneimage.com
Web: www.cattailcreekinn.com
Sue and Harold Buchman, Innkeepers

Staying in bed and breakfast inns and experiencing that personalized style of travel has been both a high-light and a focus for Sue and Harold Buchman during the past 20 years as they've traveled throughout the U.S. and abroad. Out of their love of that experience and their enjoyment of hosting travelers in their own home, the idea for a bed and breakfast grew. They designed the Cattail Creek Inn to incorporate all the special amenities and features they themselves have most enjoyed. On a carefully chosen location backing up to the golf course, with spectacular views of mountain peaks and only a block from Lake Loveland, they've created an award winning Inn that attracts both leisure and business travelers..

Cherokee Park Ranch
Box 97
Livermore, CO 80536
970-493-6522
Fax: 970-493-5802
Toll Free: 800-628-0949
Email: cpranch@gateway.net
Web: www.ranchweb.com/cherokeepark
Dick & Christine Prince

Cherokee Park Ranch's accommodations include their 110-year-old log lodge suites and six outlying cabins. All lodging units have porches with swings for you to sit upon and relax as the river flows nearby. Elk, mule deer, coyotes, and bald eagles are just a few of the native animals you may see from your front porch. They boast of splendid home cooking served family style, and they will not neglect your sweet tooth. Several cookouts during the week include steaks and ribs, but always with a chicken option. Adults also enjoy a candlelight and wine dinner one evening while the children have their own cookout. A beautiful ranch to discover on horseback!

China Clipper Inn
PO Box 801
525 2nd Street
Ouray, CO 81427
970-325-0565
Fax: 970-325-4190
Toll Free: 800-315-0565
Email: clipper@rmi.net
Web: www.chinaclipperinn.com
Earl Yarbrough, Innkeeper

The China Clipper combines the romance of an historic building while incorporating modern amenities. Generous use of well-placed windows in every room maximizes your views of the magnificent San Juan Mountains, the most dramatic setting in Colorado. Romance, relaxation and adventure await you for this perfect getaway vacation. Enjoy the spectacular setting of Ouray from the covered front porch, decks and enclosed garden. Our uniquely decorated inn, personal service and good food create an ambiance of warmth and well being. You are where you have always dreamed of being.

Colorado Trails Ranch
12161 County Road 240
Durango, CO 81301
970-247-5055
Toll Free: 800-323-3833
Email: info@coloradotrails.com
Web: www.coloradotrails.com

The ranch's origins are unique. Founded in 1960, Colorado Trails Ranch is one of the only dude/guest ranches built specifically to be a family vacation destination. Most present day guest ranches originally started as something else (i.e. working cattle ranch, hunting lodge, etc.) and later evolved into dude ranches. They have developed their recreational programs to accommodate different levels of ability, age and interests. When combined with the spectacular mountain location, great food and other activities you have a vacation that you will always remember and hopefully come back to enjoy again and again!

Coulter Lake Guest Ranch
PO Box 906
Rifle, CO 81650
970-625-1473
Toll Free: 800-858-3046
Don Hock and Russ & Susan Papke

A perfect rustic setting for summer vacations since 1936. Located twenty-one miles northeast of Rifle in the White River National Forest. The ranch offers unlimited horseback riding through aspen, spruce and meadows of wildflowers. Activities include fishing or swimming in their private lake, cookouts, square dancing, horseshoes, volleyball, hiking, 4-wheel drive trips, sing-a-longs and weekly overnight pack trips-but no regimented program. Great homecooking is the trademark of this ranch. Rafting, golf, hot mineral springs trips can arranged for a nominal amount.

Deer Valley Ranch
Box V
Nathrop, CO 81236
719-395-2353
Toll Free: 800-284-1708
Email: fun@deervalleyranch.com
Web: www.deervalleyranch.com
Woolmington and DeWalt families

Located in the heart of the Collegiate Peaks Fourteener range, The ranch faces 14,269 foot Mt. Antero, while behind is 14,197 foot Mt. Princeton. The ranch itself lies at the base of spectacular Chalk Cliffs that loom more than 1,000 feet tall. Soak in the natural hot springs pool before enjoying a delicious homecooked meal, cookout or specialty buffet. Their 50 member staff is there to look after your needs and those of your entire family. In keeping with their family atmosphere, no alcohol is allowed on the ranch property. As their guests, you are more than clients; you are guests in their home during your stay at Deer Valley Ranch.

Drowsy Water Ranch
PO Box 147A
Granby, CO 80446
970-725-3456
Toll Free: 800-845-2292
Email: dwrken@aol.com
Web: www.drowsywater.com
Ken & Randy Sue Fosha

Your owner-hosts Ken, Randy Sue, Justin and Ryan Fosha invite you to their ranch and home to enjoy the western vacation of your dreams. For over 65 years this 600 acre ranch, nestled in its own private mountain valley, has provided folks from around the world with authentic western vacations. Under the same ownership/management for 20 years, the Fosha's Drowsy Water Ranch has developed a reputation for quality Dude Ranch vacations. The Ranch has programs for children from infants to teenagers with plenty of activities for parents and grandparents alike. Singles and couples are welcomed also. All of the guest accommodations (log cabins and lodge rooms) have been completely remodeled and redecorated in recent years.

The Edwards House
402 West Mountain Avenue
Ft. Collins, CO 80521
970-493-9191
Fax: 970-484-0706
Toll Free: 800-281-9190
Email: edshouse@edwardshouse.com
Web: www.edwardshouse.com
Leslie Vogt & Greg Belcher,
Innkeepers

Renowned local architect Montezuma Fuller built the Edwards House in 1904 for Alfred Augustus Edwards, an early Colorado pioneer from Mercer, Pennsylvania. The house remained the family home of the Edwards' until 1981 when it was sold and used for offices until being converted to use as an inn. High ceilings and large leaded glass windows afford the interior a bright spaciousness that complements the antique furnishings. It is located in a quiet residential area of town within walking distance to City Park, the historic Old Town shopping and restaurant district, and the Colorado State University campus.

Elk Mountain Ranch
PO Box 910
Buena Vista, CO 81211
719-539-4430
Toll Free: 800-432-8812
Email: elkmtn@sni.net
Web: www.elkmtn.com
Tom and Sue Murphy

Elk Mountain Ranch offers a complete one-week package that includes the best activities Colorado has to offer at a very reasonable all-inclusive price. They are dedicated to excellence in accommodations and hospitality, as well as being committed to upholding the deserved reputation for a traditional western vacation experience that is unsurpassed. Elk Mountain is unique for its spectacular location, horseback rides of unmatched beauty and variety, superb menu, and intimate capacity. The Ranch is nestled among aspen and evergreen on Little Bull Creek and surrounded by a breathtaking panorama of snowcapped peaks. Accommodations include log cottages and lodge rooms, each carpeted and tastefully furnished, with daily housekeeping service.

Galena Street Mountain Inn
106 Galena Street
PO Box 417
Frisco, CO 80443
970-668-3224
Fax: 970-668-1569
Toll Free: 800-248-9138
Email: galenast@aol.com
Web: www.colorado-bnb.com/galena
Sandra and John Gilfillan,
Innkeepers

The Galena Street Inn boasts a light, spacious interior. Fourteen beautifully furnished guest rooms provide solitude, each with private bath, bedding including Scandia Down comforters, cable TV and phones with voice mail and data ports. Large windows with window seats frame mountains so close you feel you are a part of them. The variety of designs provides their guests with attractive room selections.

The Hearthstone Inn
506 North Cascade Avenue
Colorado Springs, CO 80903
719-473-4413
Fax: 719-473-1322
Toll Free: 800-521-1885
Email: hearthstone@worldnet.att.net
Web: www.hearthstoneinn.com
David and Nancy Oxenhandler,
Innkeepers

Whether for a romantic retreat, family vacation, or for business, the Hearthstone Inn provides a casual, Victorian elegance. In summer the crack of croquet balls on the manicured lawn mingles with the soft melodies of wind chimes on the shady veranda where you can relax in an oak rocking chair. The hushed whisper of the first snowfall and the crackle of pine logs in the parlor fireplace are joined by the rich aroma of fresh coffee at the end of the day. Spend a few days with us and wake to sunlight streaming through leaded glass and the tempting scents of spices–cinnamon, nutmeg, cloves–wafting from the kitchen. Now featuring in our resturant, our wonderful new French chef! Open daily to the public.

The Historic Pines Ranch
PO Box 311
Westcliffe, CO 81252
719-783-9261
Toll Free: 800-446-9462
Email: horse@historicpines.com
Web: www.historicpines.com
Dean and Casey Rusk, and Christy Veltrie

An 1890's style lodge furnished with Victorian antiques, as well as newly redecorated cabins with one to four bedrooms. Each is designed in Victorian, Country, Western or Southwest motifs. Most have King, Queen or Double beds. Activities include horseback riding, team penning, fishing in the ranches' streams, stocked pond, and in the mountain lakes, fly fishing instruction, square dancing, staff show, fishing derby, overnight pack trip, white water rafting, indoor heated pool, hot tub and sauna, cookouts, sing-along's, breakfast ride and a Saturday guest rodeo at the ranch. Three Buffet style, home-cooked hearty ranch meals per day keep their guests coming back for more. Fruit and salad bar, endless cookie/snack jars, weekly breakfast ride help to liven up the fare.

King Mountain Ranch
PO Box 497
Granby, CO 80446
970-887-2511
Fax: 970-887-9511
Toll Free: 800-476-5464
Email: hosts@kingranchresort.com
Web: www.kingranchresort.com
Jim Rea

The King Mountain Ranch is a full service Guest and Dude Ranch and Conference Retreat Center located just 90 miles northwest of Denver, Colorado near Rocky Mountain National Park. Surrounded by over one million acres of national forest and nestled in a beautiful mountain valley, the King Mountain Ranch Resort is the perfect setting for vacations, exclusive corporate retreats, and family reunions. At 9,000 ft. above sea level, the mountain setting is perfect for a variety of activities. The entire family can enjoy horseback riding, trout fishing on their private lake, swimming in the indoor pool and hot tub, skeet and trap shooting, an organized children's program, innovative cuisine, and many other recreational activities including their own bowling alley.

Lake Mancos Ranch
42688 CRN
Dept. A
Mancos, CO 81328
970-533-1190
Toll Free: 800-325-9462
Email: ranchlml@fone.net
Web: www.lakemancosranch.com
The Sehnert family

Swing up on horseback and ride among the shimmering aspens. Follow the gold panning streams to mining towns of yesteryear. Breathe deeply the fresh alpine air or settle in and watch the sunset over Sleeping Ute Mountain. Get in touch with nature in the heart of Mesa Verde Country. Fish for Colorado trout, share a horseback ride with your children and make memories to last a lifetime. This is Lake Mancos Ranch, your Home in the Southwest Colorado Mountains.

Laramie River Ranch
25777 County Road 103
Jelm, WY 82063
970-435-5716
Toll Free: 800-551-5731
Email: ranchvacation@LRRanch.com
Web: www.LRRanch.com
Bill & Krista Burleigh

Picture yourself in the majestic Rocky Mountains fishing for wild brown trout, helping our wranglers push cows between pastures, or just kicking back on the porch with a hefty glass of iced tea and a homemade cookie. You may catch a glimpse of the antelope that roam the sage-covered hillsides, the elk that range among the aspen, or moose that occasionally wander down the valley. You may even see beaver hard at work in a stream or irrigation ditch. The Laramie River Ranch offers genuine western hospitality far from the tensions of city life. Horseback riding is their specialty but they also have exceptional fly-fishing, a unique naturalist program, very comfortable accommodations, and excellent food. Come experience "the way the West was."

Latigo
Box 237
Kremmling, CO 80459
970-724-9008
Toll Free: 800-227-9655
Web: www.latigotrails.com
Yost and George families

Latigo Ranch is secluded and small (35 guests); the perfect size to create a sense of "family comin' home". They are located at 9,000 feet above sea level in an environment of vast, heavy pine and spruce forest, aspen, sagebrush, huge high meadows, streams and beaver ponds. Their riding, hiking and vistas are spectacular indeed. Whether riding horses, fly-fishing or just plain relaxing, families love Latigo. Guests rave about their food as well as their world-class hospitality.

Leadville Country Inn
127 East Eighth Street
Leadville, CO 80461
719-486-2354
Fax: 719-486-0300
Toll Free: 800-748-2354
Email: lcinn@bemail.com
Web: www.leadvillebednbreakfast.com
Maureen & Gretchen Scanlon,
Innkeepers

Just imagine the picture postcard perfect place. Plenty of snow in the winter, crisp mountain air any time of the year and flowers blooming all summer long. Welcome to Leadville, Colorado. Soak up the history of a city so wealthy that it could pave the sidewalks in front of its opera house with bricks of pure silver, in honor of a visit by President Ulysses S. Grant. In the center of all this is the Leadville Country Inn. Noted for its passion for perfection, this lovely Victorian home has everything you would expect to help you relax at the end of any day's activities. The amenities will be the highlight of your trip to the Leadville area.

Lightner Creek Inn
999 County Road 207
Durango, CO 81301
970-259-1226
Fax: 970-259-9526
Toll Free: 800-268-9804
Email: lci@frontier.net
Web: www.lightnercreekinn.com
Suzy and Stan Savage,
Innkeepers

Just five minutes to the best restaurants in town, but a million miles into a dream, the Lightner Creek Inn is situated across from the Peregrine Bird Sanctuary & adjacent to an elk preserve. Resembling a French country manor, ten exquisite guest rooms with queen or king size beds and private baths are located in the manor house. Sink into luxury for a peaceful night's sleep under down comforters, quilts or beautiful duvets. The carriage house is perfect for honeymooners or special occasions with its spacious and private suites; one with a full kitchen and nook, two with Jacuzzi tubs, and all with spectacular views.

Lost Valley Ranch
29555 Goose Creek Road
Box 70
Sedalia, CO 80135
303-647-2311
Email: lostranch@aol.com
Web: www.lostvalleyranch.com
Bob Foster family

Lost Valley is rated by AAA as a "4 diamond" property and provides western comfort in the style of "Levi Luxury." One, two and three bedroom cabin suites are cozy, comfortable and immaculately serviced. Half of the twenty-four one-to three-bedroom cabin suites are single-family structures with living rooms, oversized queen or king beds, Louis L'Amour paperbacks on the fireplace mantel, and wall-to-wall carpeting. You'll enjoy many of the niceties of home like a porch swing, plenty of over-sized towels, a refrigerator, king and queen beds, non-allergic pillows and electric coffee maker. Wood is delivered daily for your fireplace! This is ranch living at its best...and with a view you'll never forget.

The Lovelander Bed & Breakfast Inn
217 West Fourth Street
Loveland, CO 80537
970-669-0798
Fax: 970-669-0797
Toll Free: 800-459-6694
Email: love@ezlink.com
Web: www.lovelander.com
Lauren and Gary Smith, Innkeepers

The Lovelander is a rambling Victorian built in 1902 that today combines historic Victorian charm with contemporary convenience. The inn features spacious, inviting guest rooms, each with a private bath. Each room has its own distinct character with vintage iron or hardwood beds and elegant period furniture. Several luxury rooms offer fireplace, whirlpool, steam shower and/or balcony deck. A hearty gourmet breakfast is served around the handsome Empire dining table with fellow guests. Concierge service and excursion planning are available to their guests. Close proximity to many restaurants, art galleries, and the Loveland Museum makes the inn the perfect choice when staying in Loveland.

Lumber Baron Inn
2555 West 37th Avenue
Denver, CO 80211
303-477-8205
Fax: 303-477-0269
Email: stay@lumberbaron.com
Web: www.lumberbaron.com
Walter Keller, Innkeeper

In 1890, Scottish immigrant John Mouat amassed a fortune in lumber. Working with the top architects of the day, Mouat helped build Denver from a mining camp along Cherry Creek to the crown jewel of the west. His Victorian estate was set in the growing town of Highlands–geographically and morally above the wild town of Denver. Built as a home to his five children and wife, Amelia, Mouat showcased his finest wares in this 8,500 square foot home. Five elegantly apportioned guestrooms, each with private bath and phone complete the second floor. The third floor with a 20 foot pyramid ceiling and select maple floor is available for weddings, meetings, and special events today.

North Fork Ranch
Box B
Shawnee, CO 80475
303-838-9873
Toll Free: 800-843-7895
Email: northforkranch@worldnet.att.net
Web: www.northforkranch.com
Dean and Karen May

The North Fork has three cabins accommodating two to three families each that are uniquely decorated with fireplaces and private baths. The Wildhorse Lodge has six private suites all with private baths and a cabin feel. All inclusive program with scenic horseback riding, whitewater rafting, professional fly-fishing instruction with Orvis equipment, overnight pack trips, sight seeing tours, guided hiking, trap shooting, target shooting, archery, pool and hot tub, and evening entertainment such as square dancing and hayrides. A little bit country with a creative gourmet flair describes the fare. Meals are served family style, except for their farewell dinner of duck or trout. Meals include turkey, pork loin, pasta as well as their outdoor BBQ's and a steak cook out.

Old Glendevey Ranch
3219 County Road 190
Jelm, WY 82063
970-435-5701
Toll Free: 800-807-1444
Email: glendevey@aol.com
Web: www.glendevey.com
Garth and Olivia Peterson

With over 27 years' experience as professional outfitters and wilderness guides, The Petersons offer Old Glendevey Ranch as a getaway to experience the beauty and bounty of the wilderness while enjoying the comforts and fun of a ranch. Their ranch is small by choice. They can accommodate a maximum of 18 guests so that each one can experience the freedom to play and enjoy the splendors of Colorado's majestic Rocky Mountains. Their offerings are many; horseback riding, fishing, breakfast rides, hayrides, barbecue cookouts. They also specialize in luxurious backcountry pack trips for a true wilderness experience.

Powderhorn Guest Ranch
Powderhorn, CO 81243
970-641-0220
Toll Free: 800-786-1220
Email: powguest@rmi.net
Web: www.powderhornguestranch.com
Greg and Shelly Williams

From late May until early October you will enjoy this friendly, personal ranch. The Powderhorn Guest Ranch offers an authentic, Western dude ranch vacation. Located high in the Colorado Rocky Mountains, the Ranch itself is secluded and private, nestled in the Powderhorn Valley, adjacent to the Powderhorn Primitive Wilderness Area. The ranch is family owned and operated and activities are geared to all ages. A vacation at the Powderhorn Ranch is like staying with family; by the end of your week you will have made fast friends of the owners, staff and other guests. The Powderhorn Guest Ranch is adjacent to over 1.4 million acres of uninhabited wilderness and forests. Their closest neighbors are cattle ranches. It is this seclusion that allows them to offer a personal, unforgettable Colorado adventure.

The Queen Anne Bed & Breakfast Inn
2147-51 Tremont Place
Denver, CO 80205
303-296-6666
Fax: 303-296-2151
Toll Free: 800-432-4667
(USA/Canada ex 303/720)
Email: travelinfo@queenannebnb.com
Web: www.queenannebnb.com
The King Family, Innkeepers

Denver's premier urban bed and breakfast inn since January 1987, the Queen Anne has 14 guest rooms. Of these, four are two-room gallery suites named for famous painters of bygone days (Audubon, Calder, Remington and Rockwell) and showing selected examples of their work. There are 10 double rooms. All are individually decorated with period antiques and have private baths, direct dial telephones, writing desks, data lines, piped in chamber music, fresh flowers and growing plants. The hot breakfast (in bed if you wish) and an evening beverage hour with Colorado wines are included.

Rainbow Trout Ranch
PO Box 458
Antonito, CO 81120
719-376-5659
Toll Free: 800-633-3397
Web: www.rainbowtroutranch.com
Doug, Linda, Dave and Jane Van Berkum

Rainbow Trout Ranch is a very special place for a unique summer vacation. It combines the best of the Colorado Rockies and the enchantment of northern New Mexico. Located in the beautiful secluded Conejos (Co-nay-hos) River valley at 9,000 feet, the ranch features vast amounts of unspoiled country in which to ride, hike, fish and ponder. It is perfect for both adults and children, with great horses, exceptional fishing, swimming, children's programs, day trips to Taos, white water rafting and the chance to ride the Cumbres and Toltec, America's longest and highest narrow-gauge steam train. Enjoy the atmosphere of their rustic log cabins and feast on wonderful homecooked meals. A historic ranch surrounded by the Rio Grande National Forest, they are within easy access of Albuquerque, Denver, Colorado Springs or Alamosa.

Rawah Ranch
Glendevey CO Rt. C
11447 N. CR 103
Jelm, WY 82063
970-435-5715
Toll Free: 800-820-3152
Web: www.rawah.com
Kunz & Zirzow families

Colorado's Rawah Ranch is a special place 8,400 feet high in the Rockies, just south of the Wyoming border. A stunning spot in the secluded, wildlife-rich Laramie River Valley, it adjoins the 76,000-acre Rawah Wilderness Area with its snowcapped peaks and the 200,000 plus acres of Roosevelt National Forest. Rawah's meals (cowboy-style with a flair) are served in the lodge dining room. Steaks and chicken grilled over aspen, plenty of fresh fruit and vegetables, home-baked breads and mouthwatering desserts. Their weekly Lantern Light Banquet and always-available between-meal snacks are just samples of ranch cooking. Their guests complain the food is too good.

Romantic RiverSong
PO Box 1910
Estes Park, CO 80517
970-586-4666
Fax: 970-577-0699
Email: riversng@frii.com
Web: www.romanticriversong.com
and www.coloradogetaways.com
Sue and Gary Mansfield,
Innkeepers

The inn is at the end of a country lane on 27 wooded acres and offers a rushing trout stream, gentle hiking trails with rock benches to enjoy the breathtaking panorama of snow-capped peaks in adjacent Rocky Mountain National Park. You will awaken in the morning to the rich aroma of freshly brewed coffee and just-out-of-the-oven rolls and breads. As you wrap yourself in one of their robes you might catch a glimpse of the sunrise casting a rosy glow on the mountain peaks. After breakfast, you can enjoy exploring the wildflower-adorned hillside or picnicking on a rock while you contemplate the beautiful view.

San Juan Guest Ranch
2882 County Road 23
Ridgway, CO 81432
970-626-5360
Toll Free: 800-331-3015
Email: sjgr@rmi.net
Web: www.sjgr.com
Pat, Scott & Kelly MacTiernan

San Juan Guest Ranch has been providing guests with a quality dude ranch experience in the Colorado San Juan Mountains for nearly 30 years. They understand the value their guests place on their travel vacation, and their only goal is to make this the best vacation your family has ever had. By keeping the guest numbers low and the level of service high, they can give you the getaway you deserve. Jerry Hulse, L.A. Times Travel Writer, said that the ranch has "an intimacy that's contagious." They strive to maintain this atmosphere for the guests, even if they can enjoy it for only one week.

The San Sophia
PO Box 1825
330 West Pacific Avenue
Telluride, CO 81435
970-728-3001
Fax: 970-728-6226
Toll Free: 800-537-4781
Email: san_sophia@infozone.org
Web: www.sansophia.com
Alicia Bixby & Keith Hampton,
Innkeepers

As you walk through the stained glass front door and into the lobby, the subdued desert pastels and teal carpeting imply a feeling of quiet elegance. You'll stroll through the building toward your room; all of which are named after former gold and silver mines in the local area. The dining area has huge windows focused up valley toward the 12,000 foot peaks of Ajax and Telluride Mountain. During the Summer, Ingram Falls (Colorado's second tallest waterfall) offers a spectacular a view from the dining room and East Dining Deck.

The Sardy House Hotel
128 East Main Street
Aspen, CO 81611
970-920-2525
Fax: 970-920-4478
Toll Free: 800-321-3457
Email: hotlsard@rof.net
Web: www.aspen.com/sardylenado
Kim Allen and Lake McLain,
Innkeepers

There are certain places in the world of inordinate and particular beauty, and among them is Aspen, Colorado. There is something of civilization and something of wilderness, something of tomorrow and something of yesterday. The Sardy House is in the heart of Aspen, within easy walking distance of all their exciting shops and restaurants, the Music Festival in the summer, and the free skier shuttle in the winter. They will be happy to arrange all of your leisure activities, and suggest special events from hot air ballooning to dog sled rides, white water rafting to high country jeeping, dinner theatre to deep powder snowcat skiing.

Sky Corral Ranch
8233 Old Flowers Road
Bellvue, CO 80512
970-484-1362
Toll Free: 888-323-2531
Email: jocon72553@aol.com
Web: www.skycorral.com
Justin & Karen O'Connor

Their smaller capacity (only 30 lucky guests) provides an intimate, friendly, family atmosphere for sharing the many activities and adventures available during your stay. Come relax and make new friends from around the world. They have a variety of accommodations to suit your family. Choose from one, two or three bedroom cabins, as well as lodge rooms. Each cabin has a deck and is uniquely situated to face the lake. All their beautiful accommodations have private baths. Their program is on the American plan and includes three generous meals daily, spacious accommodations, transfers, and all ranch activities.

Skyline Ranch
Box 67
Telluride, CO 81435
970-728-3757
Toll Free: 888-754-1126
Email: skyline-ranch@toski.com
Web: www.ranchweb.com/skyline
The Farny family

At Skyline Ranch they are committed to sharing with you a special spirit they call "Mountain Joy". You will awaken to sunlit views of 14,000 foot peaks, take a breakfast ride through flower filled meadows or fly fish their three trout filled lakes. Perhaps you are a little more adventurous and would like to explore the San Juan Mountains by jeep, horseback, mountain bike or on foot. Some are more attracted to a visit to nearby Anasazi ruins at world famous Mesa Verde National Park. Afterwards, you can relax in the comfort of classic country lodging back at the ranch. Scrumptious meals and a congenial staff who help to make every stay at Skyline a memorable holiday round out your vacation.

Sod Buster Inn
1221 9th Avenue
Greeley, CO 80631
970-392-1221
Fax: 970-392-1222
Toll Free: 888-300-1221
Email: sodbuster@ctos.com
Web: www.colorado-bnb.com/sodbuster
Bill and LeeAnn Sterling, Innkeepers

The Inn is located on the Historic Monroe Corridor between downtown Greeley and the University of Northern Colorado). The unique octagonal, three-story structure with off-street parking was built in 1997. Though each room offers separate and distinct antique and classic country furnishings, all rooms offer the following amenities: Either a king or queen bed, desk with modem port and telephone, direct cable to main office printer, comfortable seating, reading lamps and private bath (some baths offer jetted tubs, while others have old fashioned claw foot tubs or soaker tubs). A first floor room has been designed to assist guests who have special needs. Each room has its own individual climate controls.

St. Elmo Hotel
PO Box 667
426 Main Street
Ouray, CO 81427
970-325-4951
Fax: 970-325-0348
Email: steh@rmi.net
Web: www.stelmohotel.com
Dan and Sandy Lingenfelter,
Innkeepers

The St. Elmo Hotel is a lovingly restored turn-of-the-century inn located in the heart of Ouray, a national historic district. Decorated with Victorian flair and full of period antiques, this 9-room bed and breakfast delights guests with a wine and cheese social hour every afternoon in the cozy parlor and a full buffet breakfast every morning served in the sunny breakfast room. After spending the day discovering a new hiking trail or the fine shops in the area, a soak in the outdoor hot tub is a great way to relax while surrounded by the beautiful San Juan Mountains.

The Stanley Hotel
333 Wonderview Avenue
PO Box 1767
Estes Park, CO 80517
(970) 586-3371
Toll Free: 800-976-1377
Fax: (970) 586-4964
Web: www.stanleyhotel.com

Built between 1906 and 1909 by F. O. Stanley of Stanley Steamer fame, The Stanley Hotel presents a modern window on a grand past. Perched on a hilltop above the picturesque mountain town of Estes Park, The Stanley Hotel boasts glorious views of Rocky Mountain National Park. In line with its grand past, the hotel offers its guests luxurious accommodations and the finest in cuisine. The Stanley has won numerous awards and has been entered into the National Register of Historic Places. It has also been designated an Historic District unto itself, an honor rarely bestowed. Due to its unique ambiance and architecture the hotel has been featured in such films as *The Shining* and *Dumb and Dumber*. It has also played host to such exalted personages as the Emperor and Empress of Japan, actors Jim Carey, Jeff Daniels and Lauren Holly, as well as best-selling horror author Stephen King.

Sundance Trail Ranch
17931 Red Feather Lakes Road
Red Feather Lakes, CO 80545
970-224-1222
Toll Free: 800-357-4930
Email: SundanceTr@aol.com
Web: www.SundanceTrail.com
Ellen and Dan Morin

Sundance offers extraordinary lodge and cabin suites for up to seven families or twenty-five guests. These professionally decorated, wheel-chair friendly suites have private baths, private outdoor entrances and decks, daily maid service, and are ideal for families and groups alike. All suites include AM-FM radios, refrigerators and individual coffee service. Whether it's breakfast cookouts, steak barbecues, lunch on the trail or picnicking under the pines, meal time is special. The ranch serves up excellent fare. Meals are hearty western, served family style, with homemade breads and desserts...always delicious.

Sylvan Dale Guest Ranch
2939 N. County Road 31D
Loveland, CO 80538
970-667-3915
Fax: 970-635-9336
Toll Free: 877-667-3999
Web: www.sylvandale.com
The Jessup Family

Sylvan Dale is nestled in a peaceful river valley at the mouth of Colorado's Big Thompson Canyon between Estes Park and Fort Collins, Colorado. The main ranch is at an elevation of 5,325 feet, rising to 7,500 feet at Cow Camp and Cedar Park Meadows. Established in the 1920's Sylvan Dale is still a working cattle and horse ranch as well as a full service dude ranch. They are open all year and offer summer vacation packages, bed & breakfast stays, facilities for business meetings and retreats, group picnics, weddings, family reunions and private celebrations. Sylvan Dale Guest Ranch is an easy hour's drive from Denver, located just West of Loveland on the way to Estes Park and not far from Boulder, Colorado.

**Vista Verde Ranch
Box 465
Steamboat Springs, CO 80477
970-879-3858
Toll Free: 800-526-7433
Web: www.vistaverde.com
John and Suzanne Munn**

Vista Verde style is first-class and friendly, whether their guests elect to stay in a private cabin or a deluxe lodge room. Cabins are furnished with beautiful antiques, relaxing chairs, and soft down comforters. They include one, two or three bedrooms, a living room, 2 baths, snack bar, woodstove and each has a private hot tub. Their tastefully decorated lodge rooms offer comfort and convenience, including a snack bar and balcony, not to mention spectacular views of the ranch. Three bountiful meals per day are prepared by their talented, award-winning chefs and served in their inviting lodge, on the sun deck or on the trail.

**Waunita Hot Springs Ranch
8007 County Road 887
Box 7D
Gunnison, CO 81230
970-641-1266
Email: WHSranch@csn.net
Web: www.waunita.com
The Pringle Family**

Waunita Hot Springs Ranch, located high in the Colorado Rockies at an elevation of 8,946 feet is 10 miles west of the Continental Divide. The ranch is surrounded by Gunnison National Forest land and summer pasture. U.S. Forest Service permits and private leases enable them to ride on pasture and otherwise enjoy the use of thousands of acres in eastern Gunnison County. Buildings at the ranch are a wonderful combination of new comfort and old charm, spacious and cozy. Carpeted, paneled guest rooms have private baths, and most have queen beds, bunks and doubles for the kids. The deck spa and 35 x 90 foot swimming pool are both fed by crystal clear hot springs. The pool is one of the largest private pools in Western Colorado.

Whistling Acres Ranch
PO Box 88CD
Paonia, CO 81428
970-527-4560
Toll Free: 800-346-1420
Email: wranch050@aol.com
Web: www.whistlingacres.com

Whistling Acres (a working cattle ranch) is located in a beautiful mountain valley at an altitude of 6,200 feet adjacent to the Gunnison National Forest and the West Elk Wilderness area. Montrose (one hour away) and Grand Junction, Colorado (90 minutes away) both have airports with connecting flights from all over the nation. Spring, Summer, Winter, or Fall, Whistling Acres Ranch is the ideal Colorado vacation spot for the whole family with only a 3-day minimum stay. Come for the food, the fun, and an unforgettable vacation adventure. You'll have a "Whistling good time" at Whistling Acres!

Wilderness Trails Ranch
1766 CR 302R
Durango, CO 81301 (winter)
23486 CR 501R
Bayfield, CO 81122 (summer)
970-247-0722
Fax: 970-247-1006
Toll Free: 800-527-2624
Web: www.wildernesstrails.com
The Roberts Family

Welcome to Wilderness Trails Ranch, a perfect blend of the past and present. Since 1970 the Roberts family has been introducing guests to their spectacular mountain valley and western heritage. You may be looking for a perfect family vacation or honeymoon spot. They invite grandparents traveling with grandchildren, couples or singles to visit their ranch near Durango in southwestern Colorado. A family reunion at WTR will be remembered long after everyone returns home.

The Wyman Hotel and Inn
PO Box 780
1371 Greene Street
Silverton, CO 81433
970-387-5372
Fax: 970-387-5745
Toll Free: 800-609-7845
Email: thewyman@frontier.net
Web: www.thewyman.com
Lorraine and Tom Lewis,
Innkeepers

The Wyman is located in the heart of the majestic San Juan Mountains of southwestern Colorado. All rooms have Queen or King size beds and are furnished with turn of the century antiques. Located at an elevation of 9,318 feet, air conditioning is not necessary. Each room has a private bathroom, telephone, TV/VCR, and a ceiling fan. The Wyman offers you the privacy of a hotel along with the ambiance of a bed & breakfast. There is both a Sitting Room and a Keeping Room for their guests to gather and meet new friends. Gift certificates are available at any time of the year to give to that special someone.

Meats

Barbequed Meat Loaf

Mix meat loaf ingredients in a bowl. Form into either 1 large loaf or 6 individual loaves. Place in a baking dish.

Mix together the sauce ingredients in a bowl. Pour over the meat and bake at 350 degrees for 45 minutes. Serve warm.

Temperature: 350 degrees
Cooking time: 45 minutes
Yields: 6 servings

- 1 pound lean ground beef
- 1 egg, beaten
- $\frac{1}{4}$ cup green pepper, chopped
- $\frac{1}{4}$ cup onion, chopped
- $\frac{1}{2}$ cup bread crumbs
- 1 teaspoon salt
- 1 teaspoon chili powder
- 1 tablespoon Worcestershire sauce
- $\frac{1}{4}$ cup milk

Sauce-
- $\frac{1}{2}$ cup catsup
- $\frac{1}{2}$ cup water
- 1 teaspoon chili powder
- 1 teaspoon brown sugar

Boeuf Bourguignon
(Beef Burgundy)

Temperature: 425 and 325 degrees
Cooking time: 2 to 3 hours
Yields: 4 servings
Can be stored for 4 to 5 days refrigerated

3 pounds chuck filet
8 cloves garlic, sliced
3 cups Burgundy wine
1 bouquet garni
4 slices thick bacon, diced
2 tablespoons butter
2 tablespoons extra virgin olive oil
3 tablespoons flour
2 teaspoons salt
1 teaspoon fresh ground black pepper
1 ½ teaspoons fresh thyme, chopped fine
2 bay leaves
1 to 2 cups beef stock
1 ½ pounds small mushrooms, stems trimmed
12 small white pearl onions
12 small red pearl onions
3 tablespoons butter
Salt and fresh ground black pepper

Cut beef into 1-inch cubes and dry on paper towels. In a large bowl place beef cubes, garlic and bouquet garni; cover with wine and refrigerate overnight.

Remove the beef cubes from the marinade and air dry for at least 2 hours, reserving the marinade. Preheat oven to 425 degrees. In a heavy skillet, heat butter and olive oil; cook the bacon until lightly browned. Remove with slotted spoon to a heavy, lidded casserole. In the same skillet, brown the beef a few pieces at a time on all sides, adding more butter and olive oil if necessary. As the beef cubes are done, remove to the casserole. On the stovetop, turn heat very low under casserole. Sprinkle flour on the beef cubes, toss gently, and cook until flour is absorbed. Place the casserole uncovered in the oven and cook for 4 to 5 minutes, then toss and cook 5 minutes more to totally sear the meat. Reduce oven temperature to 325 degrees. Return the casserole to the top of the stove, and pour in the reserved wine marinade, salt, pepper, bay leaves and half of the beef stock. Bring to a simmer and then cover. Place covered casserole in oven and cook for 1 ½ to 2 hours, or until meat is almost tender. Check frequently to make sure that liquid has not boiled away. Add more burgundy and beef stock as necessary.

Boeuf Bourguignon (continued)

Peel the pearl onions and make a small "X" in the root end to eliminate separation. Clean and dry the small mushrooms keeping the trimmed stems in place. Lightly sauté the onions and mushrooms together in butter. Sprinkle with salt and pepper. Add the onions and mushrooms to the stew and cook $\frac{1}{2}$ to $\frac{3}{4}$ hour longer, or until meat and vegetables are tender. Check frequently to make sure that liquid has not boiled away. Add more burgundy and beef stock as necessary.

Garnish with fresh rosemary. Serve in large bowls accompanied by fresh hot French bread.

Note: Use a reasonably good, but inexpensive wine. The cheaper the wine, the better, just as long as it's a Burgundy.

Beef Stroganoff

**Cooking time: 30 to 45
  minutes**
Yields: 8 to 10 servings

2 pounds sirloin steak
**2 cups fresh mushrooms,
  sliced**
¼ cup butter
½ cup onion, diced
2 to 3 cloves of garlic
14 ounces beef broth
2 cups sour cream
¼ cup white wine
Salt and pepper to taste
Cooked egg noodles

Slice the steak into ¼-inch strips. Melt the butter in a large skillet, then sauté the onion and minced garlic until tender. Brown the steak strips in the skillet at this time. Remove the steak from the skillet and set aside. Add the mushrooms and broth to the skillet, cover and simmer until mushrooms are almost cooked. Add the steak, sour cream, white wine, salt and pepper. Stir and bring to a boil. Serve over egg noodles garnished with parsley sprigs. Good with candied carrots, rolls and a light dessert.

There Once Was a Family of Four

*There once was a family of four
who strolled into Sundance's door
They asked to go ride
and none of them died
but all of their rearends were sore*

Beef Teriyaki

Bring the cup of water to a boil. Add in the ginger and garlic. Reduce the heat and let the mixture simmer for 10 minutes. Add the soy sauce and brown sugar, mixing thoroughly. Simmer until the sugar dissolves. Add the sherry and stir. Remove from heat and let the mixture cool completely.

Marinate the sirloin in the cooled teriyaki sauce for 24 hours. Remove the beef from the marinade and grill or broil approximately 20 minutes on each side. Use a meat thermometer for best results. Thinly slice the beef against the grain before serving.

To use the teriyaki as a glaze to serve with the beef, prepare another batch as before. Just before you add the sherry, mix the sherry with some cornstarch. Add to the mixture. This should thicken the teriyaki sauce to the consistency of a glaze.

Garnish the beef with chopped parsley and the glaze. Serve with mixed vegetables and new potatoes.

Cooking time: 40 to 60 minutes
Yields: 4 to 6 servings

2 pounds top sirloin
1 cup water
$1/4$ teaspoon fresh ginger, grated
1 teaspoon garlic, crushed
$1/2$ cup soy sauce
$1/2$ cup brown sugar
1 tablespoon cooking sherry
1 tablespoon corn starch

Beer Brisket

Temperature: 350 degrees
Cooking time: 5 to 6
hours
Yields: 20 to 25 servings

1 medium onion per
brisket
Salt and pepper to taste

Sauce (for each 4 pounds
of meat)-
¼ cup chili sauce
1 clove of garlic
2 tablespoons flour
2 tablespoons brown
sugar
1, 12-ounce can of beer

Trim the fat from the brisket. Season with salt and pepper. Place meat in a baking pan, cover with onion slices (one onion per brisket). Combine the sauce ingredients and pour over meat. Cover brisket with foil. Bake at 350 degrees for 5 to 6 hours. Uncover during the last 30 minutes and baste with juices.

"We found everything–the food, accommodations, staff, riding lessons, fishing and even the weather to be outstanding and far beyond our expectations."

166

Citrus Encrusted Pork Tenderloin

Preheat the oven to 325 degrees. Trim the tenderloin, making sure that you take off the silver. Mix together the lemon and orange zest, garlic and pepper and spread out on a cutting board. Roll the tenderloin in the coating, making sure to cover all of the tenderloin. Place on a roasting rack in the oven for 35 to 40 minutes.

Temperature: 325 degrees
Cooking time: 35 to 40 minutes
Yields: 6 servings

1 pork tenderloin
Zest of 2 lemons
Zest of 1 orange
1 tablespoon garlic, minced
1 tablespoon cracked black pepper
1 tablespoon fresh thyme

"The fabulous food, our beautiful room and the wonderful surrounding facilities can't be beat. But more important is the feeling of being one big family."

Chili Encrusted Pork Tenderloin

Temperature: 350 degrees
Cooking time: 12 to 15
minutes
Yields: 4 servings

3 pork tenderloins,
  about 12 to 14 ounces
  each
Red Pepper Coulis, see
  recipe
Yellow Pepper Coulis,
  see recipe
Basmati Rice, see recipe
Ancho Chili Crust, see
  recipe
24 spears of Asparagus

Bring a pot of water to a boil to cook the asparagus. Meanwhile, clean the tenderloins of all fat and silver skin. Roll in the chili crust until completely coated; set aside.

Heat a large sauté pan with about 4 tablespoons of corn or safflower oil. Once very hot, add the tenderloins. Cook for approximately 3 minutes and rotate. Repeat until all sides of the pork have been nicely seared. Place pan into preheated 350 degree oven for 12 to 15 minutes for medium to medium well done meat.

Once the pork has been in the oven for about 7 minutes, add the asparagus to the boiling water. Remove the pork from the oven and place on a cutting board to rest. Place a spoonful of the rice in the center of each plate. Ladle about 1 ounce of the Red Pepper Coulis in 3 places around the rice, spacing them evenly. Repeat the process for the Yellow Pepper Coulis placing 1 ounce next to each pool of the red pepper sauce.

Cut the tapered end off one of the pork tenderloins, be sure that it is a nice flat cut so the pork will stand up properly. About 1 $\frac{1}{2}$ to 2 inches up from the initial cut make another cut, but this one at a 45-degree angle. Move up the pork another 1 $\frac{1}{2}$ to 2 inches and make a straight cut; you should see a pattern here.

Chili Encrusted Pork Tenderloin (continued)

Repeat this process for all the pork. You will need 12 angled pieces, 3 for each plate.

Once the pork is cut, place each piece in the middle of the pools of sauce; there should be a red side and a yellow side with the pork in the middle. Place two spears of asparagus in between each of the 3 pools of sauce for the final touch.

Jalapeño Pork Roast

Temperature: 350 degrees
Cooking time: 2 ½ to 3 hours
Yields: 13 to 16 servings
Can be stored for 4 days.

1 pork tenderloin, 5 to 6 pounds
5 to 6 scallions, sliced thin
3 to 4 Jalapeño peppers, sliced thin
1, 12 ounce-can frozen orange juice concentrate
16 ounces Italian salad dressing

Butterfly the pork roast. Add the scallions and Jalapenos in the middle. Tie the roast back together. Mix the thawed orange juice concentrate and Italian salad dressing together. Marinate the roast in juice and dressing mixture overnight or for at least 5 to 6 hours, turning occasionally. Remove the roast from the marinade and reserve the liquid. Put the roast on a rack in a roasting pan. Bake in preheated 350 degree oven, basting with marinade occasionally, for 2 ½ to 3 hours or until a meat thermometer reads 160 to 170 degrees.

Pan Seared Beef Tenderloin

Season the meat with salt and pepper. Get a sauté pan smoking hot with the olive oil in it. Add the beef being careful not to burn yourself. Sear about 4 minutes per side or until nicely seared. Finish cooking to desired temperature in the oven. Just before the beef is done, place 4 plates in the oven for 45 seconds to heat them.

In the center of each plate pile about 1 cup of the Wild Mushroom Risotto. Place the beef on top. Rub 1 tablespoon of the Black Olive Pesto on top of each then top that with about 1 ½ tablespoons of the Oven Roasted Tomato Relish. Toss the Haricot Verts with butter, salt and pepper and place randomly around the plate.

"Fantastic food!"

Sharon
Niwot, CO

Yields: 4 servings

4, 6-ounce Filet Mignons
Salt and pepper to taste
1 tablespoon olive oil
4 tablespoons Black
   Olive Pesto, see recipe
6 tablespoons Oven
   Roasted Tomato
   Relish, see recipe
4 cups Wild Mushroom
   Risotto, see recipe
Haricot Verts, see recipe

Pork Tenderloin with Honey-Mustard Sauce

Temperature: 375 degrees
Cooking time: 2 hours to
marinate pork, 40 min-
utes to cook
Yields: 4 servings
Both the pork and the
sauce can be stored in
the refrigerator.

1 pound pork tenderloin

Marinade-
  ¼ cup stone-ground
  mustard
  2 tablespoons honey
  1 tablespoon sherry
  vinegar or white wine
  vinegar
  Cooking spray

Sauce-
  2 tablespoons honey
  1 tablespoon sherry
  vinegar or white wine
  vinegar
  ¾ cup chicken broth
  ¼ cup sherry
  2 tablespoons shallot,
  minced
  1 tablespoon stone
  ground mustard

Combine the tenderloin and the marinade ingredients in a large zip-top plastic bag. Seal and marinate in the refrigerator for 2 hours, turning occasionally. Remove the tenderloin from the bag, reserving the marinade.

Preheat the oven to 375 degrees. Place the tenderloin on a broiler pan coated with cooking spray. Insert a meat thermometer into the thickest portion of the meat. Bake at 375 degrees for 40 minutes or until thermometer registers 160 degrees (slightly pink). Let stand for a couple of minutes before slicing.

To prepare the sauce, combine the reserved marinade and the sauce ingredients in a small saucepan; bring to a boil. Reduce heat to medium; cook 15 minutes more. Serve each slice of pork with 3 tablespoons of sauce.

"Our first family trip west was everything we could have hoped for–and more! Your hospitality is beyond superlatives."

Scott & Kris
Conyers, GA

Spinach and Fontina
Stuffed Beef Tenderloin

Make a 1-inch cut across the grain of each tenderloin, about halfway through, to make a pocket. Sauté the spinach in white truffle oil over medium-high heat until wilted. Stuff each tenderloin with ⅛ cup Fontina and ¼ of the sautéed spinach. Season with salt and pepper. Grill over medium-high heat until done to desired temperature.

An elegant recipe, ideal for holiday entertaining. Serve with a full bodied Cabernet Sauvignon.

Temperature: stovetop, medium-high
Yields: 4 servings

4, 6-ounce beef tenderloin filets
1 pound fresh spinach
½ cup Fontina, grated
1 tablespoon white truffle oil (available in specialty markets)
Salt and pepper to taste

Swiss Cream Steak

Temperature: stovetop, medium
Cooking time: 50 minutes
Yields: 6 servings

6 tablespoons cooking oil
2 cups onions, sliced
2 pounds round steak
½ cup flour
1 tablespoon salt
1 teaspoon black pepper
1 teaspoon paprika
1 cup water
½ cup sour cream

In a large skillet, sauté the onions in 4 tablespoons cooking oil. Remove from the skillet and set aside. Cut the steak into ½-inch thick strips and dredge in flour seasoned with salt, pepper and paprika. Add 2 tablespoons cooking oil to the skillet and brown the meat well on both sides. Mix in the sautéed onions, water and sour cream until blended. Cover and cook over medium heat, until the meat is tender, about 40 minutes. Uncover and cook until the sauce thickens, about 10 minutes.

Teriyaki Pork Loin

Mix all the ingredients well. Place the pork loin in a roasting pan and pour the marinade over the top. Marinate for at least 4 hours in the refrigerator.

Slowly grill the loin over charcoal for 2 hours, turning frequently. Slice thinly and top with any remaining sauce. Garnish with fresh rosemary.

Temperature: grill
Cooking time: 2 hours
Yields: 8 to 10 servings

1 pork tenderloin
2 tablespoons brown
  sugar
2 cloves garlic, minced
2 tablespoons dry sherry
4 tablespoons onion,
  minced
1 teaspoon ginger
1 cup soy sauce

Veal Piccata

Yields: 4 servings

2 pounds fillet of veal
¼ cup all purpose flour
4 tablespoons butter
3 tablespoons extra
virgin olive oil
½ teaspoon salt
½ teaspoon fresh
ground black pepper
¼ cup dry white wine
¼ cup fresh lemon
juice
2 tablespoons capers
Parsley chopped for
garnish

Cut the veal into ½-inch thick slices and pound very thin. You can buy very thin cut veal in the market, but it should be clear, not marbled. Dredge the veal slices in the flour and shake off excess. In a large heavy skillet, melt the butter and olive oil together. Over medium-high heat brown the veal on both sides and cook for about 4 minutes. Shake the skillet; add the wine, lemon juice, capers, and salt and pepper. Cook for about 1 minute while stirring. Sprinkle chopped parsley on top of veal and serve.

Serve with steamed broccoli and roasted sweet potatoes.

"Everything is wonderful here: The atmosphere, the rooms, the breakfast. We took a lot of pictures so that we will never forget the hotel!"

THE WYMAN HOTEL & INN

Baked Fowl in Sherry Cream Sauce

Clean the birds, cut up and skin, if desired. Dip in flour and brown in a buttered skillet. Set aside. Sauté the mushrooms, almonds, onion and celery in butter. Place the birds in a Dutch oven and pour sautéed mixture and sherry over them. Cover and bake at 350 degrees for 1 hour.

After 1 hour, add the cream and pepper. Cover and bake an additional 30 minutes or until birds are tender. The cream makes gravy. There is no need to stir. You may serve right out of the Dutch oven.

This works great outdoors in a cast iron Dutch oven. Produces very tender and flavorful birds.

"There are not enough words to express to you how wonderful our honeymoon at Sky Corral Guest Ranch was. It was absolutely perfect!"

Sonja and Bill

Temperature: 350 degrees
Cooking time: 1 ½ to 2 hours
Yields: 4 to 8 servings

2 pheasants, or 4 quail, or 8 duck, grouse or dove breasts
Seasoned flour
3 tablespoons butter
½ pound fresh mushrooms, sliced or canned mushroom soup
⅓ to ½ cup almonds, sliced
½ onion, chopped
3 stalks celery, chopped
1 cup sherry
1 pint heavy cream
1 teaspoon salt (optional)

Blackened Buffalo Quesadilla

Temperature: 350 degrees
Cooking time: 30 minutes
Yields: 4 servings

**4, 6-ounce buffalo
  medallions**
**Blackened seasoning to
  taste**
24 ounces of Feta cheese
4 flour tortillas
2 tomatoes, sliced
Sour cream
Salsa
Cilantro

Preheat the oven to 350 degrees. Season the buffalo medallions with the blackened seasoning and bake in the oven to the desired doneness. Buffalo generally tastes better cooked medium rare to medium. Remove from the oven and slice. Spread the feta cheese generously around the flour tortilla. Place buffalo slices across half of each tortilla. Fold the tortillas in half and grill to desired crispness. Garnish with salsa, cilantro and a dollop of sour cream.

A western twist on a Mexican favorite. With its low fat and cholesterol, excellent flavor and old west appeal, buffalo meat works great for King Mountain Ranch's gourmet western cuisine.

"I do not believe we could have enjoyed our stay any more–anywhere!"

Aylesbury, Bucks, England

Braised Rabbit Southwest

Divide the rabbit into quarters and cut out the tenderloin. Save the carcass for stock. This can be done ahead by a butcher.

Combine the cumin, chili powder, coriander, garlic, cayenne and oil. Rub the rabbit thoroughly with the spice mixture. Season with salt and pepper, then dredge in the flour.

Note: You may freeze the rabbit after it is breaded. It stores well, and the freezing holds the breading together when the time comes to use it.

Preheat the oven to 400 degrees. In a large sauté pan, heat the oil until the pan is smoky hot. Brown the rabbit pieces, except for the tenderloin. Add the vegetables and deglaze with red wine. Reduce the mixture for approximately 5 minutes. Add the glace, chilies and water to almost cover. Cover the pan and place in the oven for 2 hours or until the meat easily pulls off the bone. Garnish with celeriac chips.

Rabbit has a wonderful flavor that makes it a favorite in Europe. Our guests enjoy the unique combination of this traditional dish with fresh flavors from the nearby deserts of the southwest.

Temperature: 400 degrees
Cooking time: 2 hours
Yields: 4 servings

2 whole rabbits (may substitute 3 pounds chicken legs and thighs)
1 tablespoon cumin
$\frac{1}{2}$ teaspoon chili powder
$\frac{1}{2}$ teaspoon coriander
$\frac{1}{2}$ teaspoon garlic
1 teaspoon cayenne pepper
3 tablespoons oil
1 cup flour
$\frac{1}{2}$ large onion, diced
1 carrot, diced
2 ripe Roma tomatoes, diced
$\frac{1}{4}$ cup celery root, diced
$\frac{1}{4}$ cup red wine
Glace de Viande (available in specialty food stores)
2 Serrano chilies
Water to cover rabbit
Salt and pepper
Celeriac chips

Celeriac Chips

Temperature: 300 degrees

4 cups oil
1 bulb celery root
Salt and pepper

Heat oil in a wok to 300 degrees. Clean the celery root and slice thinly into chips. Note: A mandolin helps when slicing thin slices.

Fry the chips until golden brown. Drain on a paper towel and season with salt and pepper.

"Telluride's most talked about inn, The San Sophia...the best place to stay in town."

Best Places to Stay in the Rocky Mountains

Crispy Sea Bass

Combine all the fish marinade ingredients in a saucepan and simmer for 5 minutes. Remove the herbs and allow the marinade to cool.

Let the fish soak in the marinade for 5 minutes before cooking. Cook the fish in a heavy skillet with a little oil. Sear both sides, and then remove from the skillet. Place the fish in a roasting pan in a preheated oven and cook for about 5 minutes at 350 degrees. Garnish with red pepper brunoise.

Serve with Lemongrass Mashed Potatoes, Carrot Ginger Sauce, Wasabi Pesto, some fried yams and a few blanched enoki mushrooms.

Temperature: 350 degrees
Cooking time: 5 minutes
 in the oven
Yields: 1 serving

 6 ounce sea bass fillet
 Red pepper brunoise
  garnish

Fish Marinade-
 2 sprigs mint
 3 sprigs cilantro
 2 cups teriyaki sauce
 1 tablespoons sambal
  oelek (chili sauce)

Hallelujah Halibut

Temperature: 425 degrees
Cooking time: 20 to 25
  minutes
Yields: 12 servings

1 cup mayonnaise
1 cup sour cream
4 teaspoons flour
1 tablespoon lemon juice
2 tablespoons minced
  onion
$1/4$ teaspoon cayenne
  pepper
1 cup Cheddar cheese,
  shredded
4 pounds halibut steaks

In a bowl, mix all of the ingredients, except for the fish, together. Spread the mixture on top of the fish. Place fish in a baking pan and bake at 425 degrees for 20 to 25 minutes.

"I felt spoiled at each meal."

Hot Crab Open Faces

Mix the crabmeat, mayonnaise, cream cheese, egg yolk, onion, mustard and salt together in a bowl. Spread the mixture on the muffin halves. Arrange the halves on a broiler pan and broil 2 to 3 minutes, until the top is golden brown.

Garnish with sliced hard-boiled eggs, tomatoes or avocados, depending upon whether it is being served for brunch or lunch.

"After becoming used to the homogenous appearance of hotels, regardless of their names, being in the Abriendo Inn's beautiful home setting was rejuvenating, nourishing and the best way to prepare for a busy tomorrow where business would require thinking on one's feet with a clear mind."

Cheryl
Minneapolis, MN

Temperature: broil
Cooking time: 2 to 3
  minutes
Yields: 6 ervings

7 $\frac{1}{2}$ ounces of flaked
  crabmeat, fresh or
  canned
$\frac{1}{4}$ cup mayonnaise
3 ounces of cream cheese
1 egg yolk
1 teaspoon onion, finely
  chopped
$\frac{1}{4}$ teaspoon prepared
  mustard
$\frac{1}{8}$ teaspoon salt
6 English muffin halves
Hard-boiled eggs,
  tomatoes or avocados
  (optional)

Pistachio Crusted Ruby Red Trout

Temperature: medium
Cooking time: 7 to 8
minutes
Yields: 4 servings

4, 4-ounce red trout
filets
Salt and white pepper
1 cup flour
2 eggs, beaten
2 tablespoons water
1 cup ground pistachios
4 tablespoons butter

Salad-
4 large handfuls of
mixed greens
4 teaspoons Dijon
mustard
4 teaspoons balsamic
vinegar
2 tablespoons olive oil
Salt and pepper to taste

Clean the trout of any excess fat or bone. Season with salt and white pepper. Dredge in the flour, and then shake off the excess. Mix the water with the beaten egg to make an egg wash. Dip the fish into the egg wash and then dredge the flesh-side in the pistachios. Heat the butter over medium heat in a sauté pan. Sauté the nut covered side of the trout for 4 minutes, until the nuts are a light golden brown. Flip the trout and sauté for another 3 to 4 minutes until done. Actual time depends on thickness of filet.

Combine the mustard, vinegar, oil, salt and pepper in a large bowl. Add the mixed greens and toss. To serve, place one handful of greens on each plate. Place trout over greens with nut side up.

A festive entre that could also be served as part of a Holiday party buffet. A crisp, fresh Sauvignon Blanc with nice acid will complete the presentation.

Rocky Mountain Rainbow Trout with Shrimp Florentine Stuffing

For the Florentine Stuffing, thaw the spinach; squeeze to remove excess moisture. Melt the butter and whisk in the flour. Slowly add the milk, chicken stock and seasonings. Cook and whisk until thickened. Add the spinach and canned shrimp; continue cooking over low heat, stirring constantly, about 5 minutes.

Rinse and dry the trout inside and out. Spray the cooking pan; arrange the trout in the pan. Fill with stuffing; place 4 or 5 fresh shrimp in stuffing (as appropriate). Place 3 pats of butter on each trout and cover with 3 lemon slices. Place in pre-heated oven and bake for 25 to 30 minutes.

Garnish with fresh whole dill weed. Serve with baby carrots.

"What a wonderful belated birthday! Jim's dinner was decadent! Once again the Castle Marne made our vacation memorable. We hope to return soon."

Virgil and Robby

Temperature: 350 degrees
Cooking time: 25 to 30 minutes
Yields: 4 servings

4, 8-ounce Rainbow Trout, with heads and tails
12 lemon slices
12 butter pats

Florentine Stuffing-
1 10-ounce package frozen chopped spinach
1, 4 ½-ounce can small shrimp, drained
¼ pound fresh salad shrimp
2 tablespoons butter
2 tablespoons flour
½ cup chicken stock
½ cup light cream
Onion salt and white pepper to taste
1 tablespoon grated Parmesan cheese (optional)

Sautéed Halibut

Yields: 4 servings

4, 6-ounce Halibut fillets
½ cup flour seasoned
with salt, pepper,
thyme and granulated
garlic
5 tablespoons olive oil
12 ounces fresh Baby
Spinach, washed
thoroughly
Basil Mashed Potatoes,
see recipe
Tomato, Artichoke,
Garlic and Kalamata
Vinaigrette, see recipe
Garlic Chips, see recipe

Heat an appropriate sized sauté pan over high heat. Add 3 tablespoons of the Olive oil. Dredge the fish in the flour and spice mixture, shaking off the excess. When the oil is hot, add the fish service side down. Let cook until the fish attains a nice golden brown color. Remove from heat and place in a preheated 350 degree oven to finish (about 5 minutes).

While the fish is cooking heat another sauté pan with the 2 remaining tablespoons of olive oil in it. When very hot, add the spinach and toss to promote even cooking. This should be a very quick process, we are only trying to quick cook it.

For service, place the desired amount of Basil Mashed Potatoes in the center of the plate. Top with the fish. Spoon some of the Tomato, Artichoke, Garlic and Kalamata Vinaigrette over the top and around the plate, being sure to get the chunks on the plate. Place three piles of the Baby Spinach, spaced evenly around the fish. Top the fish with the Garlic Chips and place the optional fried basil leaves around the plate.

Shrimp Dijon

Preparation should begin 15 minutes before serving time. Shell and de-vein the shrimp. Melt $\frac{1}{4}$ cup (4 tablespoons) of the butter in a skillet. Add the shrimp, parsley, pimento, Worcestershire sauce and lemon juice. Sauté for 5 to 10 minutes Melt the remaining butter in a saucepan or skillet; add the flour and stir until smooth. Gradually stir in the milk. Add the pepper, dry mustard, and shredded cheese. Cook over low heat until the sauce thickens. Add the shrimp mixture to the cheese sauce and serve over rice.

Yields: 5 servings

1 $\frac{1}{2}$ pounds shrimp
7 tablespoons butter
2 teaspoons fresh
   parsley
1 small can pimento
1 teaspoon
   Worcestershire sauce
1 tablespoon lemon juice
1 tablespoon flour
1 cup milk
$\frac{1}{4}$ teaspoon pepper
1 teaspoon dry mustard
$\frac{1}{2}$ pound Cheddar
   cheese, shredded

Baked Chicken Breast Stuffed With Sautéed Spinach and Mushrooms

Temperature: 350 degrees
Cooking time: 45 minutes
Yields: 4 servings

4 ounces butter
4 ounces onion, minced
48 ounces mushrooms, minced
48 ounces spinach
32 ounces bread crumbs
16 ounces heavy cream
4 boneless, skinless chicken breasts
16 ounces dry white wine
Salt and pepper to taste
Flour

Preheat the oven to 350 degrees. To prepare the stuffing, sauté the onions in the butter, and then add the mushrooms and spinach. Sauté briefly. Add the wine and cook until the contents are reduced by half. Add the bread crumbs and cook for 3 minutes. Add the heavy cream and bring to a boil. Remove the mixture from the heat and reserve.

Flatten the chicken breasts with a mallet, and then season with salt and pepper. Place two tablespoons of the stuffing onto the flattened chicken breasts, then roll each up tight. Dredge the rolled chicken in the flour and pan fry in clarified butter until golden brown on all sides. Finish the chicken in the oven. Garnish with fresh, colorful vegetables and serve.

Best when served with fresh vegetables and fresh baked bread.

When deciding on a nightly menu, Chef DeNittis likes to provide options that please everyone. This dish is familiar and comfortable, yet unexpectedly delicious and impeccably presented.

Chicken 'n Rice

Preheat the oven to 350 degrees for metal or 325 degrees for a glass baking dish. Layer the rice into the bottom of a greased 9 x 13-inch pan or casserole dish. Salt and pepper the chicken to taste and place on top of the rice. Sprinkle the dried onion soup mix over the chicken. Pour the diluted soup mixture over the chicken. Bake for 1 hour.

Remove from oven and garnish with parsley. Serve with tossed salad and fresh baked rolls.

"We are still filled with warmth, smiles, a few extra pounds and all the wonderful and unforgettable memories of your ranch."

Temperature: 325 to 350 degrees
Cooking time: 1 hour
Yields: 6 servings

1 cup dry rice
1 package dried onion soup mix
1, 10 ¾-ounce can cream of chicken, celery or mushroom soup, mixed with 1 ½ cans of water
1 frying chicken or favorite pieces
Salt and pepper to taste

Chicken Wontons

Temperature: 400 degrees
Cooking time: 10 to 12
  minutes
Yields: 48 wontons

1 package boneless,
  skinless chicken
  breasts
$\frac{1}{2}$ onion, diced
Oil
$\frac{1}{2}$ cup green chilies,
  diced
$\frac{1}{2}$ loose cup fresh
  cilantro, chopped
1 teaspoon cumin
2 cups Monterey Jack
  cheese, grated
1 cup Cheddar cheese,
  grated
$\frac{1}{2}$ teaspoon pepper
1 package wonton sheets

In a fry pan, sauté the chicken, diced onions and cumin, using just enough oil to coat the bottom of the pan. Cook over low heat, until the chicken is well cooked throughout. Set aside to cool. Chop the cilantro and grate the cheeses, then mix with the green chilies and pepper. Shred the chicken with a fork and add to the spiced cheese mixture.

Lightly grease a mini-muffin pan and place a wonton sheet in each cup. Fill with the chicken/cheese mixture and place in a preheated 400 degree oven. Bake for 10 to 12 minutes or until the edges of the wontons are golden brown.

Remove from the oven and top each wonton with a dollop of sour cream. Garnish with diced tomato, sliced black olive, cilantro leaf or whatever your creativity dictates.

Cornish Game Hens with Wild Plum Glaze and Seasoned Rice Stuffing

Rinse and dry the hens, inside and out. Sprinkle salt in the cavity of each hen. Fold the wings akimbo. Tie the drumsticks together. Place in a baking pan that has been sprayed with vegetable spray; baste the hens with butter. Preheat the oven to 350 degrees. Place the baking pan in the oven. While baking, turn the hens occasionally and re-baste. 5 minutes before serving, spread the plum jam on the hens with a pastry brush. Re-heat for 5 minutes.

Prepare seasoned rice to specifications.

To serve, un-tie the drumsticks; stuff the cavity with the prepared rice, allowing some to spill out onto plate. Garnish with fresh Sage or Thyme sprigs. Serve with orange glazed baby carrots, and fresh steamed asparagus.

A fancy and elegant entrée that is very easy to make. This is another option offered as an entrée with our candlelight dinners.

Temperature: 350 degrees
Cooking time: 25 to 30 minutes
Yields: 4 servings

4, 1 ½-pound Cornish Game Hens, thawed
Wild Plum jam
Butter for basting
1, 4-serving box of your favorite prepared seasoned rice mix.

Game Hens a l'Orange

Temperature: 325 degrees
Cooking time: 75 minutes
Yields: 2 to 4 servings

2, 1-pound game hens, thawed
2 tablespoons butter
3 ounces frozen orange juice concentrate
6 tablespoons water
1 tablespoon bottled steak sauce
1 tablespoon honey
½ teaspoon salt
½ teaspoon rosemary leaf, crumbled

Preheat the oven to 325 degrees. Cut the hens in half and brown in butter in a large skillet. Remove the birds from the skillet and set aside; keep warm. Add the orange juice concentrate, water, steak sauce, honey, salt and rosemary to the skillet and stir with the browning juices. Bring the sauce to a boil, scraping the pan to loosen the cooked bits. Place the hens in a casserole dish and pour the sauce over them. Cover and bake for 75 minutes or until the hens are tender. Remember to baste several times during the baking.

This dish is good served with wild rice.

Paprika Chicken

Preheat the oven to 350 degrees. Mix together all the ingredients. Lay out chicken on paper lined sheet pan. Brush on sauce. Turn chicken and brush on sauce onto second side. Cover with foil and bake for 1 hour. Uncover pan, baste chicken with sauce and return pan to oven for another 30 minutes.

Temperature: 350 degrees
Cooking time: 90 minutes
Yields: 20 servings

20 small to medium
  chicken breasts or
  equivalent
4 cups butter, melted
3 tablespoons garlic salt
$\frac{1}{2}$ cup paprika
Salt and pepper to taste
2 cups lemon juice
4 tablespoons brown
  sugar
$\frac{1}{2}$ cup leaf oregano

"The meals were superb. There were healthy choices at every meal. I especially appreciated the fruits and vegetables."

Pueblo Chicken On A Stick

**Temperature: low to
medium on the grill
Cooking time: 10 to 15
minutes
Yields: 9 servings**

**6 large chicken breasts
2 large bell peppers
18 button mushrooms
6 hot Pueblo chilies
3 large Roma tomatoes
1 cup lemon concentrate
½ cup onion, diced
3 tablespoons garlic
powder
3 tablespoons fresh
cilantro
1 teaspoon salt
½ teaspoon white
pepper
9 skewers**

Cube the chicken and set aside in a bowl. Cut up the bell pepper and set aside with the mushrooms in another bowl. Put all of the remaining ingredients in a blender and blend well. Pour the mixture over the chicken, cover and refrigerate overnight.

The next day, alternately place the chicken and vegetable pieces on the skewers. Cook, turning periodically until done. Garnish with sliced tomatoes and chopped cilantro.

This is served at the Abriendo Inn barbecue breakfast with an egg dish and potatoes. This is also used for lunch or dinner with other side dishes.

"Our big adventure started 23 hours before in Europe. When we arrived at the Abriendo Inn it was 'Paradise Found'! Great hospitality, wonderful rooms, marvelous food."

*Monique
Luxembourg*

Sesame Ginger Chicken

Mix the soy sauce, honey, sesame seed and ginger together in a small bowl; set aside. Flatten the chicken to approximately $\frac{1}{4}$-inch in thickness. Add the chicken to the sauce and let sit for about 30 minutes. Grill over a hot fire.

Temperature: hot on the grill
Yields: 4 servings

2 tablespoons soy sauce
2 tablespoons honey
1 tablespoon sesame seeds, toasted
$\frac{1}{2}$ teaspoon ground ginger
4 boneless chicken breasts (1 pound)

Trapper Tom's Chicken Pot Pie

Temperature: 375 degrees
Cooking time: 1 hour
Yields: 4 servings
Can be stored for 3 days
  refrigerated

5 tablespoons butter
½ cup onion, chopped
2 cloves garlic, chopped
⅓ cup flour
2 cups chicken stock
Salt and fresh ground
  black pepper
2 cups cooked chicken,
  chopped
¾ pound button
  mushrooms, sliced
2 tablespoons crumbled
  sage
2 frozen puff pastry
  squares
Water to moisten pie edge

In a medium saucepan melt the butter over medium heat. Cook the onion until tender; add garlic and sauté for 1 minute. Add flour and cook, stirring for about 1 minute without browning. Add chicken stock and cook, stirring until sauce thickens. Add salt and pepper to taste. Stir in the chicken, mushrooms and sage, remove from heat and set aside.

Preheat oven to 375 degrees.

To assemble pie: Roll out 1 pastry square to about ⅛-inch thick and place into 2-quart square baking dish. Edges should extend over sides; moisten them with water. Add chicken filling. Roll out second pastry square to the size of the baking dish and place over top. Crimp edges together. Make 4 slashes in top of pastry.

Place in the oven and bake for 1 hour. Remove from the oven and allow to cool for a few minutes. Garnish with sour cream and chives, (a small amount). Serve with a dark green salad and fresh hot French bread.

Pastas, Casseroles & Soufflés

Angel Hair Pasta with Alfredo Sauce

Cook the pasta. Heat the cream cheese, milk and butter together. Mix in the Parmesan until smooth. Pour over the pasta and serve. Garnish with Parmesan cheese or crushed garlic croutons. Serve hot with a good steak.

Cooking time: 15 minutes
Yields: 8 to 10 servings

8 ounces cream cheese
¾ cup Parmesan cheese
½ cup butter
½ cup milk, whole
  works best
Pasta of choice

"I felt like it was home!! The best vacation I've ever had!! And I've been to Europe, Mexico..Sundance has ambience, friendship, lots of beautiful scenery to enjoy while riding, great food, comfortable rooms, can't wait to get back next year!!!"

Cyril Hennum
San Diego, California

Chile Relleno Soufflé

Temperature: 300 degrees
Cooking time: 2 ½ hours
Yields: 20 servings

1, 27-ounce can diced
  green chilies
1 pound Cheddar
  cheese, grated
1 pound Monterey Jack
  cheese, grated
5 eggs
1, 14-ounce can
  evaporated milk
3 tablespoons flour
½ teaspoon salt
¼ teaspoon pepper
10 ounces enchilada
  sauce

Preheat the oven to 300 degrees. Layer a third of the diced green chilies in the bottom of a 4-quart baking dish. Cover these with a layer of Cheddar cheese. Layer in another third of the green chilies. Cover this with a layer of Jack cheese. Layer in the last of the green chilies.

Separate the eggs. Beat the yolks, and then add the evaporated milk, flour, salt, and pepper. Mix well.

In a separate bowl, beat the egg whites until stiff. Fold the whites into the yolk mixture and pour over the layered chili/cheese mixture. Bake for 2 hours, uncovered. Pour the enchilada sauce over the top and bake for an additional 30 minutes.

Fabulous Pesto with Fettuccini

Place the nuts, garlic, ¼ cup olive oil and Basil leaves in a food processor or blender; process until evenly pureed, about 15 seconds. Transfer to a bowl. Slowly stir in the cheese, salt, sun dried tomatoes, parsley and ¾ cup olive oil. Do not heat the pesto. Makes 1 ½ cups pesto, enough for 1 pound of pasta, cooked and drained. In a large bowl, toss the pasta with the pesto. Serve hot.

Helpful hint for nuttier flavor: Pine nuts may be lightly toasted in a toaster oven or in a frying pan on the stovetop.

Garnish with fresh chive blossoms. Serve with garlic bread sticks and Chianti wine. This is one of the vegetarian entrées offered with our candlelight dinners.

"This was our first B & B and WOW! We indulged ourselves in the candle-lit dinner for 2 in the dining room–we were in a food coma. What a meal! We will definitely be back. I would like to splurge and get the Presidential Suite, although I absolutely loved the Mason Room, very romantic!"

Carl & Anne

Cooking time: 5 to 7 minutes
Yields: 4 servings

- **⅔ cup pine nuts**
- **1 cup olive oil**
- **2 medium-size garlic cloves, peeled and minced**
- **3 cups fresh basil leaves, firmly packed (remove stems, wash and dry)**
- **¼ cup grated Parmesan cheese**
- **¼ cup fresh parsley, chopped**
- **½ cup sun dried tomatoes, diced**
- **1 pound fettuccine, linguine or gnocchi**

King Crab and Shrimp Noodles

Temperature: 350 degrees
Cooking time: 35 minutes
Yields: 8 servings

6 ounces crab meat,
  canned or frozen
12 cooked medium
  shrimp
2 cups fine noodles
  (angel hair), uncooked
1, 10 ½-ounce can
  cream of mushroom
  soup
½ cup mayonnaise
½ cup milk
Cheddar cheese,
  shredded

Preheat the oven to 350 degrees. Mix everything, except for the cheese, together carefully, making sure not to break up the shrimp and noodles too much. Pour into a 1 ½-quart casserole dish. Sprinkle the Cheddar cheese on top and bake for 35 minutes.

Lumber Baron Mini-Soufflés

In a prep bowl, whisk the eggs with the whipping cream and a dash of salt and pepper. Keep mixing for 1 to 2 minutes. Coat the insides of 6 individual baking tureens with a non-stick vegetable spray. Fill the tureens approximately ⅓ full with your filling ingredients. Pour the egg mixture over this filling, until the tureen is nearly full.

Place the tureens on a baking sheet (necessary to catch the overflow) and bake for 15 to 20 minutes in a 400 degree oven. The soufflés are done when they puff into a peak and some of the filling boils out. If the center is still wobbly and hasn't overflowed, they need a little more time in the oven.

Serve on a small saucer with a doily and a slice of kiwi, orange or strawberry as a garnish. Serve immediately.

These delightfully petite soufflés are quite filling, as well as pleasing to the eye. Easy to make as either vegetarian or with meat, to please all tastes.

Temperature: 400 degrees
Cooking time: 15 to 20 minutes
Yields: 6 servings

8 eggs (substitute Egg Beaters™ for low fat)
½ cup heavy whipping cream
Salt and pepper to taste

Filling-
¾ cup shredded cheese, any variety
1 cup hash browns or chopped potatoes
½ bunch green onions, diced
Ham or sausage, cut small
Fresh or frozen vegetables

Orzo with Thyme and Lemon Zest

Temperature: stovetop, medium
Yields: 8 servings

2 cups Orzo pasta
1 cup chicken stock
1 tablespoon lemon zest
2 teaspoons dried thyme
2 tablespoons butter
$\frac{1}{2}$ cup Parmesan cheese
7 teaspoons salt
$\frac{1}{2}$ teaspoon ground pepper

Set a large pan of salted water to boiling. Add the Orzo pasta and cook until al dente (approximately 8 to 10 minutes). Drain the pasta and rinse with hot water. Combine the orzo with the chicken stock, lemon zest, thyme, salt and pepper. Cook it over moderate heat, until most of the liquid is absorbed. Stir in the butter and Parmesan just prior to serving.

Portabella Mushroom Mozzarella

Pre-cook the pasta. Combine the tomato sauce, garlic, basil, oregano and red pepper flakes in a saucepan over medium heat. Once heated, set aside. Heat oil in a skillet. Press some wheat germ into the slices of mushroom and sauté over medium/high heat, turning once, about 1 ½ to 2 minutes per side. Remove from heat. Place the drained pasta in a shallow casserole dish. Spread half of the tomato sauce on top. Salt and pepper to taste. Top with some of the cheese. Layer the mushroom slices on the sauce and top with remaining sauce and cheese. Bake at 350 degrees for 15 to 20 minutes or until cheese is melted and beginning to brown.

Garnish with parsley sprigs or garlic croutons. Serve with garlic bread and Caesar salad. We often serve this as a vegetarian entrée opposite beef stroganoff or spaghetti on Italian night.

Temperature: 350 degrees
Cooking time: 15 to 20 minutes
Yields: 6 to 8 servings

1 to 2 cups chunky tomato sauce
2 to 3 cloves garlic, crushed
¼ teaspoon basil
½ teaspoon oregano
1 pinch red pepper flakes
4 large portabella mushrooms, sliced
2 tablespoons olive oil
1 tablespoon toasted wheat germ
6 to 8 ounces mozzarella cheese
Pasta of choice

Potato Casserole

Temperature: 350 degrees
Cooking time: 60 minutes
Yields: 12 to 16 servings

  Red skinned potatoes,
    boiled and sliced
  Butter
  Fresh chopped parsley
  Rosemary
  Salt and pepper to taste
  Grated white cheese
    (your choice)
  ½ cup milk

Spray a large casserole dish with a vegetable oil spray. Place a layer of sliced potatoes in the bottom of the dish. Place several pats of butter on top of the potatoes. Sprinkle part of the fresh chopped parsley, rosemary, salt, pepper and grated white cheese on top of the butter and potatoes. Place a second layer of potatoes and repeat the butter, spices and cheese.

Continue layering until the dish is nearly full. Top with the remainder of the cheese. Pour ½ cup milk over the baking dish contents. Cover with aluminum foil and bake for 30 minutes in a 350 degree oven. Remove the foil and bake uncovered for an additional 30 minutes.

Sandia Soufflé

Preheat oven to 375 degrees. Roll out one pastry square to about 1/8-inch thick and place into a 2-quart square baking dish, leaving the edges extended over the sides. Layer the cheese, onion and green chilies in the baking dish. Beat eggs; add peppers and salt. Add the egg mixture. Roll out the second pastry square to the size of baking dish. Place over top of dish and crimp edges together.

Garnish with fresh salsa and sour cream. Serve with rosemary roasted potatoes.

"Thank you for a relaxing stay in your beautiful inn–the atmosphere is so peaceful–the breakfasts special & delicious!"

Temperature: 375 degrees
Cooking time: 1 hour
Yields: 4 servings
Can be stored for 1 day refrigerated.

2 frozen puff pastry squares, thawed
8 ounces sharp Cheddar cheese, shredded
1 small onion, finely chopped
4 large roasted green chilies cut to lay flat
6 large eggs
1/4 teaspoon fresh ground black pepper
Pinch of red pepper
Pinch of salt (optional)
Water to moisten pastry edge

Scalloped Corn and Sausage

Temperature: 350 degrees
Cooking time: 90 minutes
Yields: 20 servings

3 pounds ground
  sausage
1, #10 can cream style
  corn
10 eggs, lightly beaten
1 cup milk
40 saltine crackers,
  crushed
Salt and pepper to taste

Preheat the oven to 350 degrees. Brown the sausage. Drain off the grease and set aside. Mix the corn, eggs, and milk together with a whisk. Add the crushed saltine crackers, salt and pepper and mix well, but lightly. Add the browned sausage and stir until evenly distributed. Pour into a lightly greased baking pan. Cover with foil and bake for 1 hour. Uncover and return to oven for an additional 30 minutes.

Serve with a baked potato and tossed green salad.

Shrimp and Angel Hair Pasta

Sauté the shrimp and garlic in the oil. Add the wine, sour cream, Parmesan cheese, chicken broth, basil, rosemary and red pepper flakes. Bring to a boil and simmer to let the flavors combine. Thicken slightly with cornstarch. Garnish with tomato and parsley. Serve over angel hair pasta.

This is served during our adult's only dinner in a candle-lit atmosphere. The kids have pizza with the staff out on the river porch.

"The food is good home cooking and the kids have wolfed it down."

The Asplin Family
High Wycombe, Buckinghamshire, England

Yields: 15 to 20 servings

2 to 3 pounds of shrimp
1 tablespoon garlic, minced
¼ cup cooking oil
2 to 3 cups dry white wine
2 cups sour cream
½ cup Parmesan cheese
3 cups chicken broth
2 teaspoons basil
2 teaspoons rosemary
¼ teaspoon red pepper flakes
Cornstarch
2 tomatoes, chopped
¼ cup fresh parsley, chopped
Salt and pepper to taste

Spaghetti Pie

Temperature: 350 degrees
Cooking time: 25 minutes
Yields: 6 servings

6 ounces spaghetti
2 tablespoons butter
2 eggs, beaten
⅓ cup Parmesan cheese
1 pound ground beef
1 pound pork sausage
½ cup onion, chopped
¼ cup green pepper,
   chopped
8 ounces canned
   tomatoes, cut up
6 ounces tomato paste
1 teaspoon sugar
1 teaspoon oregano
½ teaspoon garlic
1 cup cottage cheese
½ cup Mozzarella,
   shredded

Preheat the oven to 350 degrees. Cook the spaghetti; drain. Stir in the butter, eggs and Parmesan cheese. Form the mixture into a pie pan. In a skillet, cook the beef, pork, onion and green pepper until tender; drain. Stir in the tomatoes, tomato paste, sugar, garlic and oregano and continue heating. Spread the cottage cheese over the spaghetti mixture. Fill the pie with the tomato mixture. Bake uncovered for 20 minutes. Sprinkle mozzarella on top. Bake an additional 5 minutes.

"There's an old fashioned goodness to this ranch that brings to mind another century. When the world was less hurried and neighbors cared about neighbors."

J.H.
Los Angeles, California

Potatoes, Rice & Vegetables

Basil Mashed Potatoes

Peel and halve the potatoes. Place them in a large pot and cover with cold water. Bring to a boil and cook until an inserted knife meets no resistance. Let drain very well. Meanwhile, stack the leaves of basil; roll and slice in a cross cut fashion (this is called Chiffonade). Place the basil, cream and butter in a saucepot. Bring to a boil, reduce heat and let reduce slowly to allow the basil flavor to infuse into the cream. Place the potatoes on a baking sheet and then into a preheated 350 degree oven to dry, this should take about 5 minutes.

Remove the potatoes from the oven and pass through a food mill to get an even consistency. For creamier potatoes pass through a Tamis. Using an electric mixer whip together the potatoes and cream mixture. Add the cream slowly (with basil) until desired consistency is reached. Season to taste with salt and white pepper. Keep warm.

Temperature: 350 degrees
Yields: 4 servings

3 large baking potatoes
1 bunch fresh basil
1 cup heavy cream
6 tablespoons whole
 butter
Salt and pepper to taste

Basmati Rice Pilaf

Temperature: 375 degrees
Cooking time: 30 to 35
  minutes
Yields: 4 servings

  1 ½ cups white Basmati
  rice
1 bay leaf
1 branch fresh thyme
3 cups chicken stock, hot
4 tablespoons butter

Place a little butter, the rice, bay leaf and thyme in an ovenproof baking dish. Heat the chicken stock and butter together to boiling. Pour over the rice and spices. Cover with foil and place the baking dish in a preheated 375 degree oven for approximately 30 to 35 minutes. Remove and fluff with a fork. Cover and keep in a warm area until needed.

Caramelized Onions

Melt the butter over medium heat. Add the onions and cook slowly until they are evenly browned. Slowly is the key here, do not rush.

Temperature: stovetop, medium

2 medium onions cut in half then sliced as thin as possible
$1/4$ cup butter

Cattle King Potatoes

Temperature: 375 degrees
Cooking time: 1 hour
Yields: 6 to 8 servings

3 pounds of potatoes
1 clove garlic
Salt
⅓ cup butter
2 egg yolks
½ cup cream
½ pound mushrooms
¼ cup minced parsley
Pepper

Peel the potatoes. Boil with garlic and salt until tender. Meanwhile, slice and sauté mushrooms in 1 tablespoon of butter. Mash the potatoes with the remaining butter. Beat the egg yolks with the cream and mix into the potatoes along with mushrooms and parsley. Add more salt and pepper as needed. Pile in a buttered baking dish and bake at 375 degrees, until brown (about 8 to 10 minutes).

"Hi! Once again, thank you so much for a FANTASTIC week! We definitely had 'ranch withdrawals'. California seems drab after the beauty of Colorado. Well you were right when you commented on how we will leave saying 'this was the best trip I have been on'! I know I can speak for my family by saying thanks to you both and the hardworking staff. We had a wonderful, enjoyable and relaxing week. We could not speak any more highly of Elk Mountain Ranch. Thank you very much."

The Warlicks
Chevy Chase, Maryland

Fried Tomatoes

Slice the tomatoes to a thickness of $1/4$ to $1/2$-inch. Place the whisked egg in a shallow dish. Mix the flour, Parmesan, salt and pepper in a second shallow dish. Dip each tomato slice in the egg, then into the dry ingredients, coating well. Fry in a skillet with the butter and olive oil until lightly browned. Flip and cook the other side.

This makes a great appetizer. They also go well as a side dish for a hearty steak meal. Serve with ketchup or salsa.

Cooking time: 30 to 45 minutes
Yields: 2 servings per tomato

Green or very firm tomatoes
Whisked egg
$1/4$ cup flour
$1/4$ cup Parmesan cheese
Dash of salt
Dash of pepper
1 tablespoon butter
1 tablespoon olive oil

Garlic Chips

Yields: 4 servings

10 garlic cloves
Cold milk
Canola oil for frying

Using a mandolin slice the garlic cloves lengthwise as thinly as possible. Place them in a saucepan and add enough cold milk to cover. Bring just to a boil and drain. Repeat this process 3 more times. The milk leeches out a lot of the bitterness and makes it a little sweet. Once the garlic has been boiled, drain and pat dry.

Heat the canola oil to about 300 degrees. Add the garlic chips and fry until the bubbling around the edges of the garlic has subsided (about 10 to 15 minutes) and they are golden brown. Drain on paper towels.

An optional garnish is fried basil leaves. Reserve 12 nice basil leaves and once the garlic has been removed from oil, add the basil. Be very careful. The moisture in the basil leaves will pop when it hits the oil causing it to splatter. The basil will only take about 5 to 10 seconds to cook. When they become translucent remove gently and place on paper towels.

Grilled Vegetables with Balsamic Vinaigrette

Combine the vegetables and then separate evenly into two large zip-top plastic bags. Combine the first six ingredients (vinegar through garlic). Divide equally and add to the vegetables. Seal the bags and marinate in the refrigerator for 1 hour. Turn the bags several times.

Prepare the grill. Coat the grill rack with cooking spray. Remove the vegetables from the marinade and place them on the grill. Grill for about 7 minutes on each side. Baste with reserved marinade. Serve with other grilled dishes such as chicken, pork or steak.

"I would love to tell you how good a time Liz & I had, but there are no words to describe our 'perfect vacation. The family atmosphere of eating with the crew, being called by our first names, going shoeless in the lodge & square dancing makes this the most memorable vacation ever. Unfortunately, I think both of us have gained weight this week, but it tasted sooooo good doing it."

Jeff & Liz
Oxford, OH

Cooking time: 15 minutes
Yields: 10 servings
Store in a bowl covered
with plastic wrap and
refrigerate.

4 plum tomatoes, halved
1 zucchini, cut into
¼-inch slices
1 yellow squash, cut into
¼-inch slices
1 cup broccoli, cut into
large chunks
1 cup cauliflower, cut
into large chunks
1 eggplant, cut into
1-inch thick slices
1 red bell pepper, cut
into large chunks
1 onion, cut into 2-inch
wedges
Cooking spray

Marinade-
⅓ cup balsamic vinegar
3 tablespoons honey
1 ½ tablespoons olive
oil
1 teaspoon ground black
pepper
½ teaspoon salt
4 garlic cloves, minced

Haricot Verts

Temperature: stovetop, high

40 Haricot Verts
1 tablespoon Kosher salt
Butter, salt and pepper to taste

Snap the stem ends off the Haricot Verts. Bring a saucepot of water to a boil. Add the Kosher salt. Blanch the beans for about 6 minutes. If you are using them right away simply drain and toss with some butter, salt and pepper. If you are cooking them ahead of time, drain and run them under cold water to stop the cooking. Reheat in a little water, butter, salt and pepper.

Lemon Carrots

Boil the carrots in salted water until crisp and tender; drain. In a saucepan, mix the sugar, lemon juice and butter; heat to boiling. Boil for 2 to 3 minutes or until thickened. Stir in the carrots, coating well. Serve warm.

Temperature: stovetop, high
Cooking time: 20 minutes
Yield: 4 to 8 servings

2 cups baby carrots
¼ cup sugar
2 ½ tablespoons fresh lemon juice
4 tablespoons butter

"Thanks for a great week at Elk Mountain Ranch. We enjoyed meeting all of you as well as the other guests during the week. The week will be remembered for friendship, adventure, service, humor and great fun. Thank you all."

John Cathy, Jordan and Alison
Angola, IN

Lemongrass Mashed Potatoes

Temperature: stovetop, boiling

10 Idaho baking potatoes
1 quart cream
3 stalks lemongrass
¼ pound butter

Boil and mash the potatoes. Simmer the lemongrass, butter and cream for 15 minutes. Pour into the mashed potatoes. Remove the lemongrass.

Stuffed Tomatoes

Cut tomatoes in half. Scoop out the center and squeeze out the juice. Dice up the center and save the pulp. Add dressing, artichokes and crumbs to the pulp and mix together. Stuff each tomato with the dressing/crumb mixture.

Place in a buttered baking dish and bake in a 350 degree oven for 30 minutes.

"The meals were excellent in all respects. Even the pack lunches were five star quality & quantity."

Temperature: 350 degrees
Cooking time: 30 minutes
Yields: 20 servings

20 large ripe tomatoes
1 cup Italian dressing
2 pounds canned artichoke hearts, drained and cut up
2 cups Italian bread crumbs
Butter

Sweet Potato Crisp

Temperature: 350 degrees
Cooking time: 30 minutes
Yields: 10 to 12 servings

7 cups cooked sweet
  potatoes, mashed
¾ cup sugar
¾ cup margarine
2 eggs
⅓ cup milk
1 teaspoon vanilla
¾ cup margarine,
  melted
¾ cup light brown
  sugar
½ cup flour
¾ cup pecans, chopped

In a bowl, mix the potatoes, sugar, margarine, eggs, milk and vanilla until creamy. Combine the brown sugar and flour. Add the melted margarine and pecans. Place the sweet potato mixture in a large casserole dish. Cover with the brown sugar mixture. Bake in an oven that has been preheated to 350 degrees for about 30 minutes.

224

Wild Mushroom Risotto

In a large sauté pan, heat the oil. Add the rice and shallot; sauté briefly. Add the wine and let reduce until almost dry. Once the wine is almost gone begin adding the stock about ½ cup at a time, stirring constantly. When the stock is almost absorbed, add more. After about 1 ½ cups of the stock have been added, throw in the mushrooms. Continue adding stock until it's gone. Just before serving stir in cheese and finish with butter.

Note: We use Porcini, Morel and Chanterelle mushrooms. If these are unavailable or if you do not wish to pay the outrageous prices they charge, simply substitute Shiitake, Crimini and button mushrooms. All of these should be available in your local grocery store.

Yields: 4 cups

2 tablespoons olive oil
1 ½ cup Arborio rice (short grained Italian rice)
3 tablespoons shallot, minced
½ cup white wine
3 cups vegetable or chicken stock, hot
1 cup assorted wild mushrooms (porcini, chanterelle, morel etc.)
½ cup Parmesan cheese, grated
2 tablespoons butter

Zucchini Split

Temperature: 350 degrees
Cooking time: 15 to 20
  minutes

3 zucchinis
½ pound sausage
1 onion, chopped
1 egg (optional)
3 to 5 tablespoons
  mayonnaise
½ cup salsa
Parmesan cheese
½ cup bread or cracker
  crumbs (Italian style
  preferred)
Grated Cheddar cheese
Corn or English muffins

Grate the zucchinis and soften in the microwave oven. Cook the sausage, until no longer pink. In a large bowl, mix the zucchini, sausage, onion, egg, mayonnaise, salsa, cheeses and crumbs together, blending until smooth. Spread on corn or English muffins. Bake on a cookie sheet at 350 degrees for 15 to 20 minutes. You may add more Cheddar cheese the last few minutes of cooking. Sprinkle dash of paprika on top.

Sauces & Marinades

Ancho Chili Crust

Place the chilies in a preheated 350 degree oven for 10 minutes. Remove and let cool. Pull the stems off the chilies and empty the seeds. Place the chilies in a food processor with the spices and puree until medium coarse in texture.

Temperature: 350 degrees
Cooking time: 10 minutes
Yields: 1 cup

5 Ancho chilies, roasted
2 tablespoons cumin, ground
2 tablespoons granulated garlic
2 tablespoons Kosher salt

Carrot Ginger Sauce

6 ounces onion, chopped
3 ounces ginger, sliced
1 ounce garlic, minced
2 ½ pounds carrots
¼ ounce cilantro, chopped
¼ ounce mint, chopped
½ ounce lemongrass, chopped
1 tablespoon chili oil
2 tablespoons canola oil

Sweat the onion, ginger, garlic, carrots, lemongrass and herbs in the oils. Cover with cold water and simmer for 10 minutes. Puree and strain the mixture. Thicken it with cornstarch.

Red and Yellow Pepper Coulis

Yields: 2 cups

**5 red peppers, seeded
and roughly chopped**
**5 yellow peppers, seeded
and roughly chopped**
4 shallots, minced
4 tablespoons butter
2 quarts chicken stock

Melt half the butter in a medium sized sauce-pot. Add 2 of the shallots and the red peppers; sauté briefly and add 1 quart of the stock. Bring to a boil and reduce heat to medium. Simmer until peppers are very soft. Puree in a blender very well. Remove to a holding container; keep warm until used.

Repeat process for Yellow Pepper Coulis, using the remaining ingredients and the yellow peppers.

Note: For best results use an instant chicken stock. The real stuff tends to thicken as it cooks, giving you a thick and nasty final product.

Steak Marinade

Yields: 5 steaks
**Steaks can be marinated
and refrigerated a day
ahead of cooking**

¼ **cup oil**
**2 tablespoons lemon
juice**
2 tablespoons soy sauce
1 clove garlic or ½
teaspoon garlic powder
**1 teaspoon coarse
pepper**
1 teaspoon celery seed

Combine all ingredients and pour over steaks.
Cover and refrigerate until ready to be grilled.

*"Thanks so much for a wonderful vaca-
tion–our best ever! You two really know how
to show people a good time! Please extend
our gratitude to your wonderful staff. Hope
to see you again SOON!"*

Steve and Lynn
Aurora, IL

Traditional English Lemon Curd

Place all ingredients, except the butter, in a double boiler and stir until well mixed. Add the butter, cut into small pieces. Cook over medium heat, stirring continuously until thickened. Pour into clean jars and cap. Refrigerate immediately.

Serve with fruit, croissants and other sweet breads, rolls or muffins.

"We visited at least 5 different Bed & Breakfast places during our Colorado vacation. Yours stands out in our minds for its cleanliness, 'homey' feeling, and friendly staff."

Martha & Jeff

Temperature: stovetop, medium
Cooking time: 20 to 30 minutes
Yields: 4, 20-ounce jars
Store for up to one month refrigerated

12 eggs, beaten well, not stringy
1 ½ cups lemon juice (6 to 8 lemons)
1 tablespoon lemon rind, grated in small pieces
3 cups sugar
1 cup butter (2 sticks)

Wasabi Pesto

3 ounces wasabi paste
4 sprigs of cilantro
5 cloves of garlic
2 tablespoons of chili oil
2 cups of canola oil
Salt to taste

Combine all the ingredients and puree in a blender.

Desserts

Blueberry Crumb Cake

Preheat the over to 375 degrees. Grease an 8-inch springform pan; set aside. In a small bowl, combine the ingredients for the topping, using a spatula to mix. In a large bowl, cream together the butter and sugar. Add the flour baking powder and salt, mixing well alternately with milk, and the lemon juice and zest. Spread the batter into the greased pan. Finish with the crumb topping and bake in the oven for 1 hour.

Cool the cake slightly in the pan. Remove the sides and cut with a serrated knife. Serve with freshly whipped cream flavored with rum, if desired.

Temperature: 375 degrees
Cooking time: 1 hour
Yields: 6 to 8 servings

2 cups plus 2 tablespoons flour
2 teaspoons baking powder
½ teaspoon salt
¼ cup unsalted butter
¾ cup granulated sugar
1 large egg
½ cup milk
Zest and juice of 1 lemon
1 ½ pints blueberries, picked over and rinsed

Topping-
¼ cup unsalted butter
½ cup granulated sugar
⅓ cup flour
½ teaspoon nutmeg

Choco-Banana Coffee Cake

Temperature: 375 degrees
Cooking time: 45 minutes
Yields: 15 servings
Can be stored for up to 8
  weeks well wrapped in
  freezer

Batter-
  ¾ cup sugar
  ½ cup margarine,
    softened
  4 mashed ripe bananas
  ½ cup sour cream
  2 eggs
  2 cups all-purpose flour
  1 teaspoon baking soda
  ½ teaspoon salt

Filling-
  1 cup walnuts, chopped
  ¼ cup packed brown
    sugar
  2 tablespoons
    margarine, melted
  1 teaspoon ground
    cinnamon
  1 cup semi-sweet
    chocolate chips

Beat sugar and margarine in a large bowl until fluffy. Stir in the bananas, sour cream and eggs. Stir in the flour, baking soda and salt. Spoon half of the batter into a 9 x 13-inch greased pan.

Sprinkle with half of filling. Spoon the remaining batter over the filling. Sprinkle the top with the remaining filling.

Bake at 375 degrees for 45 minutes, or until a knife comes out clean when inserted into the center and the cake pulls away from the edges of the baking dish.

"I greatly enjoyed being at your B & B. I could sense the love you both have to your Innkeeper's roles."

Cowboy Coffee Chocolate Cake

Preheat oven to 350 degrees. Grease and flour a pair of 9-inch cake pans. Sift the cocoa, flour, cinnamon and baking soda together. Dissolve the coffee into water. On medium speed, beat the sugar, dressing and coffee mixture into the dry ingredients with a mixer. Divide the batter between the 2 cake pans. Bake for about 30 minutes or until a knife inserted into the center comes out clean. Cool and turn onto racks.

While the cake is cooling, mix together the ingredients for the coffee syrup. Make sure the ingredients are well blended.

To start the frosting, mix the sugar, cocoa and cinnamon. Beat $\frac{1}{4}$ cup of coffee and the butter into the dry ingredients. Add the last couple of tablespoons of coffee 1 tablespoon at a time until frosting is smooth, fairly stiff, but creamy enough to spread easily.

Once cooled, cut each cake horizontally. Brush each layer with 2 tablespoons of the coffee syrup and spread $\frac{3}{4}$ cup frosting. Assemble the layers on a cake platter and frost.

Temperature: 350 degrees
Cooking time: 35 minutes
Yields: 10 servings
Stores well covered for a couple of days.

$\frac{1}{2}$ cup cocoa
2 cups flour
1 teaspoon cinnamon
2 teaspoons baking soda
1 cup sugar
1 cup salad dressing
1 cup cold water
2 teaspoons instant
  coffee powder

Coffee Syrup-
  6 tablespoons water
  3 tablespoons sugar
  1 tablespoon instant
    coffee powder

Frosting-
  4 cups powdered sugar
  $\frac{1}{2}$ cup cocoa
  1 teaspoon cinnamon
  $\frac{1}{4}$ cup plus 2
    tablespoons coffee (use
    coffee not coffee
    powder)
  $\frac{1}{2}$ cup butter, melted

Cream Cheese Pound Cake

Temperature: 350 degrees
Cooking time: 70 minutes
Yields: 1 cake

8 ounces cream cheese, softened
1 cup margarine, softened
½ cup butter, softened
3 cups sugar
6 eggs
3 cups flour
2 tablespoons vanilla

In a large mixing bowl cream together the margarine, butter and cream cheese. Add the sugar. Beat until light and fluffy. Add the eggs to the mixture, one at a time. Stir in the vanilla. Add the flour and mix well.

Preheat the oven to 350 degrees. Grease a 10-inch tube pan and pour in the batter. Place in the oven and bake for 70 minutes or until a cake tester inserted into the middle comes out clean.

Cream Puff Cake

In a large saucepan, bring water, margarine and salt to a boil. Add flour immediately. With a wooden spoon, beat flour into the water/margarine mixture, stirring until the mixture leaves the side of the pan in a small ball (about 1 to 2 minutes). Remove from heat. Add eggs, stirring in one at a time. Turn mixture into an 8 ½ x 11-inch greased pan. Bake at 400 degrees for 20 to 25 minutes. Remove from the oven and flatten the middle with a spatula, leaving the pastry higher on the sides.

Mix filling ingredients until well blended. Spread over the cooled pastry and cover with whipped topping.

Temperature: 400 degrees
Cooking time: 20 to 25 minutes
Yields: 12 servings

Puff Pastry-
1 cup water
½ cup margarine
⅛ teaspoon salt
1 cup flour
4 eggs

Filling-
3 small packages instant pudding mix
8 ounces cream cheese, softened
2 ½ cups milk

Topping-
8-ounce carton whipped topping

Crème de Menthe Cake

Temperature: follow
  package directions
Cooking time: follow
  package directions
Yields: 15 servings
Can be stored for 2 to 4
days

1 white cake mix
3 tablespoons Crème de
  Menthe liqueur
1 jar of Hershey's
  Chocolate Shoppe
  Fudge™

Topping-
8 ounces non-dairy
  topping
3 tablespoons Crème de
  Menthe liqueur

Prepare the cake mix as per the package directions, adding 3 tablespoons of the Creme de Menthe into the batter. Bake according to mix directions and let cool for 45 minutes. Spread the fudge on top of the cake. Let cool completely.

Mix the non-dairy topping and remaining Crème de Menthe together. Spread over the top of the fudge. Refrigerate the cake.

You can also garnish the cake with shaved chocolate curls in addition to the topping above.

Fresh Apple Cake with Caramel Frosting

Preheat the oven to 375 degrees. Cream the shortening with the sugar and add the well-beaten eggs. Sift the dry ingredients together and add alternately with the apples, raisins and nuts. Bake in a greased and floured pan for 35 to 45 minutes or until a cake tester inserted into the middle comes out clean.

Combine all ingredients for the frosting in a saucepan, except for the milk, and bring to a boil. Add enough milk to give the mixture a thin paste consistency and cook for 3 minutes. Let stand. Add powdered sugar until it's thick enough to spread on the cake.

Temperature: 375 degrees
Cooking time: 35 to 45
  minutes
Yields: 8 servings

  1/2 cup shortening
  1 teaspoon cinnamon
  1 cup sugar
  3/4 teaspoon allspice
  2 eggs, well beaten
  1/2 cup cold coffee
  1 1/2 cups sifted flour
  2 cups apples, finely
    chopped
  1 teaspoon baking soda
  1 cup raisins
  3/4 teaspoon salt
  1/2 cup chopped nuts

Caramel Frosting-
  1 cup brown sugar
  1 tablespoon butter
  1 cup powdered sugar
  3 tablespoons vegetable
    shortening
  Milk

Ice Cream Cake

Temperature: 375 degrees
Cooking time: 10 to 12
  minutes
Yields: 10, 1-inch slices

4 egg yolks
⅓ cup sugar
½ teaspoon vanilla
4 egg whites
½ cup sugar
⅔ cup sifted cake flour
1 teaspoon baking
  powder
¼ teaspoon salt
¼ cup cocoa
Chocolate chip ice
  cream, softened

Beat egg yolks until they become thick and lemon-colored. Gradually beat in ⅓ cup sugar; add in vanilla. In a separate bowl, beat the egg whites until soft peaks form. Gradually add ½ cup sugar and beat until stiff peaks form. Fold yolks into egg whites. Sift together flour, baking powder and salt. Fold into egg mixture.

Spread batter evenly in greased and lightly floured 15 ½ x 10 ½ x 1-inch jelly-roll pan. Bake at 375 degrees for approximately 10 to 12 minutes.

Remove from oven and immediately loosen the sides and turn out onto a tea towel that has been sprinkled with sifted confectioner's sugar. Starting at the narrow end, roll cake and towel together; cool on a rack. Unroll the cake, spread with softened mint chocolate chip ice cream. Roll up the cake, without the towel. Place on serving dish seam side down. No altitude adjustment needed below 7,600 feet.

"You guys bent over backwards for us and we really appreciated all you did! Not only did we have a memorable time, but went away with great friendships too!"

Miriam and Tracey

Praline Cheese Cake

In a bowl, combine the graham cracker crumbs, butter and sugar. Press this mixture into an 8 or 9-inch spring form pan. Bake at 350 degrees for 10 minutes. Remove from the oven and let cool. In a separate bowl, beat together the cream cheese and brown sugar. Add the flour and eggs one at a time. Beat well. Add the vanilla and pour the batter onto the crust. Top with pecans. Bake at 350 degrees for 40 minutes. Turn off the oven, keeping the cake in the oven with the door closed for an additional 30 minutes. Remove from the oven and chill for 2 hours before serving.

Temperature: 350 degrees
Cooking time: 80 minutes
Yields: 8 servings
Can be stored for 4 to 5 days

- **1 cup graham cracker crumbs**
- **6 tablespoons butter**
- **$\frac{1}{4}$ cup sugar**
- **3, 8-ounce packages cream cheese**
- **1 $\frac{1}{2}$ cups light brown sugar**
- **1 tablespoon flour**
- **3 eggs**
- **1 $\frac{1}{2}$ teaspoons vanilla**
- **$\frac{1}{2}$ cup pecans, finely sliced**

Pumpkin Gingerbread Cake

Temperature: 350 degrees
Cooking time: 1 hour

3 cups sugar
1 cup oil
4 eggs, beaten
⅔ cup water
1 pound canned
  pumpkin
3 ½ cups all purpose
  flour
2 teaspoons baking soda
1 teaspoon salt
½ teaspoon baking
  powder
2 teaspoons ginger
1 teaspoon cinnamon
1 teaspoon nutmeg
1 teaspoon cloves
1 teaspoon allspice

Center the rack in the oven and preheat to 350 degrees. Cream the sugar, oil and eggs together in a large mixing bowl. In a separate bowl, sift the dry ingredients and the spices together. Add the sifted ingredients and the water alternately to the creamed mixture. Thoroughly mix in the pumpkin and pour the mixture into a greased bundt pan. Bake for 1 hour or until a cake tester inserted into the center comes out clean. Cool on a wire rack.

Snickers Cake

Mix the cake according to package directions. Pour half the batter into a greased and floured 9 x 13-inch pan and bake for 20 minutes at 350 degrees. Meanwhile, melt the caramel, margarine and milk together. Pour over the baked batter. Sprinkle with nuts and chocolate chips. Add the remaining batter and bake at 250 degrees for 20 minutes and then at 350 degrees for 10 minutes.

Our guests go crazy for this one and it is so easy!

**Temperature: 350 and
  250 degrees
Cooking time: 50 minutes
Yields: 15 servings
Can be stored for 1 week**

**1 German chocolate
  cake mix
1 package caramel
1 stick butter or
  margarine
$\frac{1}{3}$ cup milk
1 cup nuts, chopped
$\frac{2}{3}$ cup chocolate chips**

Sweet Potato Cheese Cake

Temperature: stovetop, low
Yields: 10 to 12 servings

1 cup vanilla wafer
   crumbs
¼ cup melted
   margarine
4 cups mini
   marshmallows
½ cup milk
1 cup mashed, cooked
   sweet potato
⅓ cup orange juice
1 teaspoon vanilla
¼ teaspoon cloves
¼ teaspoon cinnamon
1 cup whipped cream
16 ounces cream cheese,
   softened

Combine the vanilla wafer crumbs and margarine, and then press into the bottom of a 9-inch spring form pan. Melt the marshmallows with the milk in a double boiler or saucepan over low heat; stir until smooth. Chill until slightly thickened; mix until blended. Whip the potatoes with the orange juice, vanilla and spices.

Combine the softened cream cheese and potato mixture, beating until well blended and fluffy (about 3 to 5 minutes). Whip in the marshmallow mixture. Fold in the whipped cream and pour into the crust. Chill well.

"Thank you for such a beautiful job for our reception. The dining room transformed into the most enchanting, intimate atmosphere for a reception. I have recommended the inn and staff highly for any of my friends and clients who need a getaway!"

Tropical Upside-Down Breakfast Cake

Preheat oven to 350 degrees. Combine 2 tablespoons butter and brown sugar in a small bowl. Spread evenly in the bottom of a lightly greased 10-inch or larger round baking dish. Combine the mangos and pineapple; spread over the brown sugar mixture and set aside.

Combine flour, baking powder and salt in a medium mixing bowl; reserve. In a separate bowl, combine the remaining 1/2 cup butter, granulated sugar and eggs; beat by hand until creamy. Add the reserved dry ingredients, orange juice, milk, vanilla and orange zest. Beat by hand until well blended. Pour the batter over the pineapple. Bake until the top is golden and a toothpick comes out clean (about 45 to 50 minutes).

Remove from the oven and allow to cool for 15 minutes. Run a knife around the edge to loosen the sides. Cover the cake with a serving plate and flip the fruit side up. Don't lift the baking dish yet, but allow to sit for another 5 to 10 minutes. Then gently raise the edge of the baking dish with a knife and slowly raise the dish. The cake will fall out of the baking dish onto the serving plate. Any pieces still sticking can be encouraged to fall out with the use of a spatula.

Temperature: 350 degrees
Cooking time: 45 to 50 minutes
Yields: 12 servings
Can be stored overnight in refrigerator

2 tablespoons butter, softened
1 cup packed brown sugar
Meat of 2 fresh mangos, diced
1, 21-ounce can crushed pineapple, well drained
1 1/2 cups all-purpose flour
2 1/2 teaspoons baking powder
1/2 teaspoon salt
1/2 cup butter, softened
3/4 cup granulated sugar
2 eggs
1/2 cup orange juice
1/3 cup low fat milk
1/2 teaspoon vanilla extract
2 tablespoons grated orange zest

Wacky Cake

Temperature: 350 degrees
Cooking time: 35 minutes
Yields: 20 servings

Cake-
 3 cups flour
 2 cups sugar
 2 teaspoons salt
 2 teaspoons baking soda
 6 tablespoons cocoa
 2 cups water
 1 teaspoon vinegar
 1 teaspoon vanilla
 ¾ cup margarine,
  melted

Frosting-
 8 ounces cream cheese
 2 tablespoons margarine
 1 cup powdered sugar
 1 tablespoon milk
 1 teaspoon vanilla

Preheat the oven to 350 degrees. Mix together the dry cake ingredients. Add the liquids and beat until smooth. Bake in a 9 x 13-inch greased cake pan until a toothpick inserted in the middle comes out clean or for approximately 35 minutes.

To make the frosting, in a small mixing bowl, beat together the cream cheese and margarine. Add the powdered sugar and vanilla. Adjust the thickness with milk or more powdered sugar.

Often a child will come and whisper in our ear that Mom or Dad or their sister or brother is having a birthday during their stay at the ranch. This is our signal to get ready for a whole lot of fun. We then enlist the aid of the child to make a birthday cake and decorate it.

This chocolate cake recipe is very simple and tasty. Top it with a basic Cream Cheese Frosting and with just a little guidance small children have little trouble executing their first ever cake-baking endeavor. Most of the time they enlist the aid of 2 or 3 of their new buddies and the afternoon is spent making a work of art. The little wrangler's excitement is almost tangible and dinner becomes an after thought for them; forget the barbecued ribs and let's get on to the important part. We occasionally find frosting in some very unlikely places even late into the winter.

Yummy Apple-Cinnamon Cake

Preheat the oven to 350 degrees. Beat 1½ cups sugar (save ¼ cup for topping), cream cheese, butter and vanilla at medium speed of a mixer until well blended (about 4 minutes). Add the eggs, 1 at a time, beating well after each addition; set aside. In a separate bowl, combine the flour, baking powder and salt. Add the flour mixture to the creamed mixture; beat at low speed until well blended. Combine the remaining sugar and the cinnamon. Take 2 tablespoons of this mixture and mix with the chopped apples. Stir this apple mixture into the batter. Pour the batter into an 8-inch spring form greased pan (may use cooking spray). Sprinkle with the remaining cinnamon mixture (can add chopped nuts to this mixture as well).

Bake at 350 degrees for 75 minutes or until the cake pulls away from the sides of the pan. Cool and serve. Garnish with fresh apples slices. Can be served warm, but is easier to cut with serrated knife when completely cooled.

A moist cake using fresh apples that can be made with fat-free cream cheese and margarine to reduce the calories to less than 300 a serving.

Temperature: 350 degrees
Cooking time: 75 minutes
Yields: 12 servings

1 ¾ cups sugar, divided
¾ cup (6 ounces) cream cheese, softened
½ cup butter, softened
1 teaspoon vanilla extract
2 large eggs
1 ½ cups flour
1 ½ teaspoons baking powder
¼ teaspoon salt
2 teaspoons cinnamon
3 cups Rome apples (about 2 large), chopped and peeled

Chinese Chews
(Butterscotch Brownies)

Temperature: 350 degrees
Cooking time: 20 minutes
Yields: 24 servings
Can be stored for several
  days or frozen

1 stick of margarine
2 1/3 cups brown sugar
3 eggs
1 1/2 cups flour
1 teaspoon baking
  powder
1/8 teaspoon salt
1 tablespoon vanilla
1 cup chopped walnuts
Powdered sugar

Preheat the oven to 350 degrees. Cream the margarine, brown sugar and eggs together in a bowl. Add the flour, baking powder, salt and vanilla; mix by hand. Add the chopped nuts. Spread into a greased 9 x 13-inch pan. Bake for 20 minutes. Cool and dust with powdered sugar.

Hawaiian Drop Cookies

Preheat the oven to 325 degrees. Mix the flour, baking powder and salt together in a bowl. In a separate bowl, cream the shortening, sugar and flavorings together. Beat in the egg until mixture is fluffy. Blend in the pineapple and dry ingredients. Drop the batter by teaspoonfuls 3 inches apart onto an ungreased cookie sheet. Sprinkle with coconut. Bake for about 20 minutes.

Temperature: 325 degrees
Cooking time: 20 minutes
Yields: 4 ½ dozen

1 ¾ cups flour
2 teaspoons baking powder
½ teaspoon salt
⅔ cup shortening
1 cup sugar
½ teaspoon vanilla
½ teaspoon almond flavoring
1 egg
¾ cup crushed pineapple, drained
½ cup shredded coconut, chopped

No Bake Chocolate Cookies

Temperature: stovetop, boiling
Yields: 2 to 3 dozen
Keeps best in the refrigerator or a cool spot

2 cups white sugar
½ cup milk
½ cup margarine
2 tablespoons baking cocoa
3 cups quick cooking oatmeal
1 teaspoon vanilla
½ cup peanut butter

Mix the sugar, milk, margarine and cocoa in a saucepan. Cook until the mixture is well blended and boils for 1 minute. Remove from the heat. Mix in the peanut butter and stir until completely melted. Add the oatmeal and vanilla. Drop by spoonfuls onto waxed paper. Let set until firm.

Orange Drop Cookies

Cream the shortening, sugar and egg together. Stir in the orange juice and peel; set aside. Combine all the dry ingredients and mix with the creamed mixture. Drop by rounded teaspoon 2 inches apart on an ungreased baking sheet. Bake in a 400 degree oven for 8 to 10 minutes.

For the frosting, blend the sugar and margarine. Slowly stir in the orange peel and juice until smooth. Allow the cookies to cool before frosting. Makes about 4 dozen 2-inch cookies.

Temperature: 400 degrees
Cooking time: 8 to 10 minutes
Yields: about 4 dozen 2-inch cookies

⅔ cup shortening (Can use half margarine, half shortening mixture)
¾ cup sugar
1 egg
½ cup orange juice
2 tablespoons orange peel, grated
2 ¼ cups flour
½ teaspoon baking powder
½ teaspoon baking soda
½ teaspoon salt

Frosting-
2 cups powdered sugar, sifted
2 tablespoons margarine or butter
1 tablespoon orange peel, grated
2 tablespoons orange juice

Victorian Vinegar Cookies

Temperature: 300 degrees
Cooking time: 30 minutes
Yields: 4 dozen

½ cup butter
½ cup margarine
¾ cup sugar
1 tablespoon white
   vinegar
1 ¾ cups flour
½ teaspoon baking
   soda
1 cup finely chopped
   walnuts

Cream the butter and margarine together in a bowl. Add the sugar and vinegar; beat until fluffy. Sift the flour and soda together in a separate bowl and add to mixture. Stir in nuts. Drop by teaspoonfuls onto ungreased cookie sheet. Bake 30 minutes at 300 degrees.

"A lonely woman on the road, a traveler from far away to far away says: Thank you, for the safe roof you sheltered me, for the warmth and the light in the night!"

Vessele
Europe

Whoopee Pies

Preheat the oven to 375 degrees. Mix all of the cookie ingredients together in a bowl, adding them in the order given. Beat until smooth. Drop by rounded tablespoonfuls onto a cookie sheet lined with parchment paper and lightly sprayed with vegetable oil. Bake for 8 to 10 minutes. Cool before making sandwiches with the marshmallow filling.

Start the filling by creaming the shortening and powdered sugar together. Beat in the remaining ingredients. Spread between cookies.

Temperature: 375 degrees
Cooking time: 8 to 10 minutes
Yields: 2 dozen

Cookies-
1 cup butter, softened
2 cups sugar
2 eggs
1 tablespoon vanilla
2 cups water
$\frac{2}{3}$ cup non-fat dry milk
4 cups flour
1 teaspoon baking powder
1 tablespoon baking soda
1 teaspoon salt
1 cup sifted cocoa

Marshmallow Filling-
1 cup shortening
4 cups powdered sugar
2 cups marshmallow whip
2 teaspoons vanilla
2 to 3 tablespoons milk

Bailey's Ice Cream

Yields: 1 gallon

6 eggs
¾ cup coffee flakes
1 quart whipping cream
2 quarts Irish cream
 coffee creamer
¼ cup Bailey's Irish
 Cream™ liqueur
½ cup Karo™ syrup
Milk to fill to 1 gallon

In a bowl, beat the eggs, until fluffy. Add the Karo™ and coffee flakes. Add in the whipping cream, coffee creamer and liqueur. Pour into an ice cream freezer and add milk to 1 gallon. Freeze according to manufacturer's directions.

Baked Alaska San Sophia

Cut the brownies into circles using a 2 ½ to 3-inch biscuit cutter. Place 1 brownie in the center of each of 4 dessert size plates. Top each brownie with ¼ cup fresh berries. Using an ice cream scoop, scoop out a large half ball of ice cream (approximately ½ cup). Place the ice cream on top of the berries, pushing it down gently to cover berries.

To start the meringue, use an electric mixer to beat the egg whites in a very large mixing bowl until tripled in volume. With the mixer still running, slowly add the sugar. Continue beating until stiff and glossy (approximately 4 to 5 minutes).

Fill the pastry bag with meringue and decoratively pipe over the ice cream and brownie. Starting at the bottom, work around the brownie and ice cream, building to the top until covered completely. With a torch or a very hot broiler, brown the outside and serve immediately.

With the addition of fresh berries, this traditional favorite offers an elegant finish.

Temperature: broil
Yields: 4 servings

1 brownie recipe
1 pint vanilla (or other favorite flavor) ice cream
½ pint blackberries (or other favorite seasonal berry)

Meringue-
16 egg whites
4 cups sugar

Special Equipment Needs-
Blowtorch or broiler
Large ice cream scoop
Pastry bag with large star tip

THE SAN SOPHIA

Cuervo Gold Tequila Parfait

Temperature: freezing
Yields: 6 servings
Can be stored frozen

6 egg yolks
2 ounces sugar
1 ½ ounces honey
3 egg whites
1 ½ ounces sugar
18 ounces whipped
cream
6 ¼ ounces sour mix
5 ounces Cuervo Gold™
tequila
1 ounce Grand
Marnier™

Whip the egg yolks, 2 ounces of sugar and honey for 10 to 15 minutes or until ribbon texture appears. Add egg whites and 1 ½ ounces of sugar until a stiff peak texture appears.

In a separate bowl, whip the cream to the same stiff peak texture. Gently fold all ingredients together. Place in a freezable container. Freeze for at least 2 hours prior to serving. Garnish with a mint leaf and almond tulle.

Lemon Ice Cream

Mix the flour, sugar, lemon extract and juice, whipping cream and Half & Half™ in a large bowl. Pour into an ice cream freezer. Add enough milk to fill the freezer to 1 gallon. Proceed according to the freezer directions.

Yields: 1 gallon

2 tablespoons flour
4 cups sugar
1 teaspoon lemon
  extract
8 fresh lemons, squeezed
3 cartons whipping
  cream
3 cartons Half & Half™
Milk to fill to 1 gallon

The Knave's Chocolate Truffles

Yields: about 34 truffles

**8 ounces semisweet
chocolate ships
2 squares (1 ounce each)
unsweetened chocolate,
chopped
1 ½ cups powdered
sugar
½ cup butter, softened
2 tablespoons B & B™
liqueur (other flavored
liqueurs may be substi-
tuted)**

Melt the chocolate chips and unsweetened chocolate in a heavy, small saucepan over low heat, stirring constantly. Set aside to let the chocolate cool. Combine the powdered sugar butter and liqueur in a bowl. Beat with an electric mixer. Beat in the cooled chocolate, until smooth. Refrigerate about 30 minutes or until the mixture is the consistency of fudge and can be shaped into balls.

Shape the mixture into 1-inch balls by rolling in the palms of your hands. Roll the truffles in chocolate sprinkles, cocoa, chopped nuts or cookie crumbs to add flavor and prevent the truffles from melting in your fingers. You can also try drizzling melted milk chocolate over the rolled truffles for a pretty effect. Decadently delicious!

We serve these at Tea Time, Luncheons and with coffee after our Candlelight Dinners

"Our night at the Castle Marne will be a memory that will last a lifetime! Snow is falling in Denver, the holiday season fills the air here and the smells from the kitchen are mouthwatering. This is life as it should be."

Bill & Hillary

Velveeta Cheese Fudge

In the microwave oven, heat the cheese, margarine and vanilla until melted. While this is melting, mix the powdered sugar, cocoa and nuts together in a large pan or bowl. Pour the cheese mixture into the sugar and mix thoroughly with your hands. You will feel the sugar dissolve. Spread into 2 or 3 buttered 9 x 13-inch pans; chill and slice. This fudge freezes beautifully and is fun to make. No one will be able to guess what the secret ingredient is!

Temperature: microwave

1 pound Velveeta™ cheese
1 pound margarine
1 tablespoon vanilla
4 pounds powdered sugar
1 cup cocoa
2 to 3 cups chopped nuts

"Thank you for such a beautiful job for our reception. The dining room transformed into the most enchanting, intimate atmosphere for a reception. I have recommended the inn and staff highly for any of my friends and clients who need a getaway!"

Brownie-Cherry Cobbler

Temperature: 350 degrees
Cooking time: 45 minutes
Yields: 20 servings

Cherry Mixture-
  16 ounces tart pie
    cherries
  1 cup sugar
  3 tablespoons tapioca
  ½ teaspoon almond
    extract

Brownie Mixture-
  4 squares of
    unsweetened chocolate
  ¾ cup butter
  2 cups sugar
  3 eggs
  1 teaspoon vanilla
  1 cup flour

Mix together the ingredients for the cherry mixture in a saucepan and heat to boiling. Boil for about 5 minutes. Pour into a greased 9 x 13-inch pan.

Melt the chocolate and butter together. Stir sugar into the mixture. Add in the eggs and vanilla and mix until well blended. Stir in the flour. Pour the brownie mixture on top of the cherry mixture. Bake at 350 degrees for approximately 45 minutes.

Garnish with a sprinkle of chopped nuts on top. I usually serve it upside down (with the cherries on top), so I usually don't bother to add the nuts. If you are serving it upside down and hot, plop a scoop of ice cream on top. Great after a short hike up the mountain.

This recipe was first created for the delight of a guest on the highly restrictive gluten-free diet. On that occasion we substituted a gluten-free brownie mix for the brownie layer. No one guessed that it was not a normal dessert. This guest was thrilled to be able to enjoy dessert with the rest of her family and the other guests. This dessert has been mentioned in several of the cowboy poems our guests write and the recipe is requested frequently.

Coconut Pie

Combine all the ingredients, in order, in a blender. Mix until smooth. Pour the mixture into a greased 10-inch pie pan. Bake for 45 minutes at 350 degrees, until a tester inserted into the middle comes out clean. This pie makes its own crust.

Temperature: 350 degrees
Cooking time: 45 minutes
Yields: 8 slices

4 eggs
1 ¾ cups sugar
½ cup flour
2 cups milk
¼ cup melted butter
1 ½ cups coconut
1 teaspoon vanilla

"Our stay here was delightful...like stepping back in time–so many unique details, we loved them all."

Marilyn & Duncan
Pueblo, CO

AWARD
WINNER

Crème Brulee

Temperature: 400 degrees
Cooking time: 45 minutes
  or until set
Yields: 7 servings

1 quart heavy cream
Dash of vanilla
¾ cup sugar
10 egg yolks

Preheat the oven to 400 degrees. Scald the cream and vanilla, then mix in the sugar and eggs. Mix well. Fill 7 ramekins (5-ounce size) and place on a sheet pan. Place the pan in the oven. Add water to fill the pan. Bake in water bath at 400 degrees for 45 minutes or until set.

Garnish with fresh fruit or fruit sauce.

Key Lime Pie

Combine the milk and limeade. Gently fold in the whipped topping and the food coloring. Pile high in the crust and freeze overnight. Top with whipped cream.

Recipe may easily be doubled if you cannot find a small can of limeade or you may use half the can of limeade. Drink the rest!

Yields: 1 pie

1 chocolate or graham cracker crust
1 can sweetened condensed milk
1 small can frozen limeade, thawed
16 ounces size frozen, whipped topping, thawed
Green food coloring - use just enough for a light green tint

Southern Apple Cream Pie

Temperature: 400 degrees
Cooking time: 40 minutes
Yields: 8 servings

1 unbaked pie shell

Filling-
2 cups chopped apples
¾ cup sugar
2 tablespoons flour
1 cup buttermilk or sour cream
1 egg, beaten
½ teaspoon vanilla

Topping-
½ cup sugar
1 teaspoon cinnamon
2 ounces butter
5 teaspoons flour

Preheat the oven to 400 degrees. Mix the apples, sugar and flour together thoroughly. Add the buttermilk (or sour cream), egg and vanilla. Pour into the pie shell. Bake for 30 minutes.

Mix the topping ingredients. After the pie has baked for 30 minutes, remove it from the oven and sprinkle the topping over it. Replace in oven and bake for an additional 10 minutes. Allow to cool.

"Thank you so much for the wonderful week we spent at Colorado Trails Ranch. Our family, all 13 of us, agreed that it was the best vacation ever and we would like to do it again."

Betty
Wichita, Kansas

Locator

1) Abriendo Inn
   Pueblo, Colorado
2) Allaire Timbers Inn
   Breckenridge, Colorado
3) Alpine Mountain Ranch
   Allenspark, Colorado
4) The Alps Boulder Canyon Inn
   Boulder, Colorado
5) Aspen Canyon Ranch
   Parshall, Colorado
6) Bar Lazy J Guest Ranch
   Parshall, Colorado
7) Black Bear Inn
   Vail, Colorado
8) The Briar Rose
   Boulder, Colorado
9) C Lazy U Ranch
   Granby, Colorado
10) Castle Marne
    Denver, Colorado
11) Cattail Creek Inn
    Loveland, Colorado
12) Cherokee Park Ranch
    Livermore, Colorado
13) China Clipper Inn
    Ouray, Colorado
14) Colorado Trails Ranch
    Durango, Colorado
15) Coulter Lake Guest Ranch
    Rifle, Colorado

16) Deer Valley Ranch
    Nathrop, Colorado
17) Drowsy Water Ranch
    Granby, Colorado
18) The Edwards House
    Fort Collins, Colorado
19) Elk Mountain Ranch
    Buena Vista, Colorado
20) Galena Street Mountain Inn
    Frisco, Colorado
21) The Hearthstone Inn
    Colorado Springs, Colorado
22) The Historic Pines Ranch
    Westcliffe, Colorado
23) King Mountain Ranch
    Granby, Colorado
24) Lake Mancos Ranch
    Mancos, Colorado
25) Laramie River Ranch
    Jelm, Wyoming
26) Latigo Ranch
    Kremmling, Colorado
27) Leadville Country Inn
    Leadville, Colorado
28) Lightner Creek Inn
    Durango, Colorado
29) Lost Valley Ranch
    Sedalia, Colorado
30) The Lovelander Bed & Breakfast Inn
    Loveland, Colorado

Locator

31) Lumber Baron Inn
   Denver, Colorado
32) North Fork Ranch
   Shawnee, Colorado
33) Old Glendevey Ranch
   Glendevey, Colorado
34) Powderhorn Guest Ranch
   Powderhorn, Colorado
35) Queen Anne Bed & Breakfast Inn
   Denver, Colorado
36) Rainbow Trout Ranch
   Antonito, Colorado
37) Rawah Ranch
   Glendevey, Colorado
38) Romantic RiverSong
   Estes Park, Colorado
39) San Juan Guest Ranch
   Ridgway, Colorado
40) The San Sophia
   Telluride, Colorado
41) The Sardy House Hotel
   Aspen, Colorado
42) Sky Corral Ranch
   Bellvue, Colorado
43) Skyline Ranch
   Telluride, Colorado
44) Sod Buster Inn
   Greeley, Colorado
45) St. Elmo Hotel
   Ouray, Colorado

46) The Stanley Hotel
   Estes Park, Colorado
47) Sundance Trail Ranch
   Red Feather Lakes, Colorado
48) Sylvan Dale Guest Ranch
   Loveland, Colorado
49) Vista Verde Ranch
   Steamboat Springs, Colorado
50) Waunita Hot Springs Ranch
   Gunnison, Colorado
51) Whistling Acres Ranch
   Paonia, Colorado
52) Wilderness Trails Ranch
   Durango, Colorado
53) The Wyman Hotel & Inn
   Silverton, Colorado

Locator

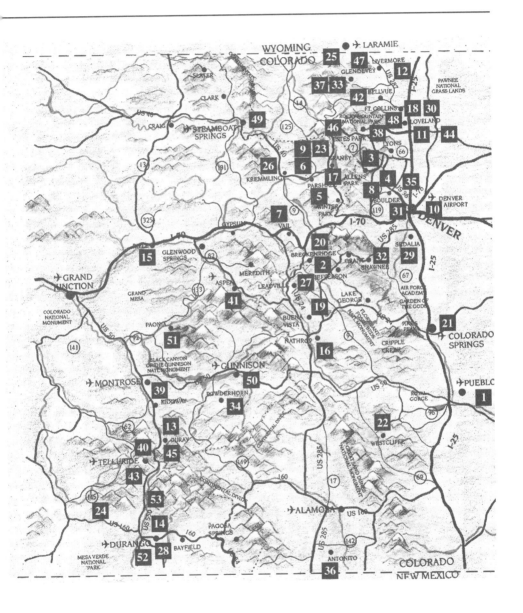

Index

Index

Index

Index

Index

Index

Index

Index

Pantry Press

3547 E. Arapahoe Road, #J224
Greenwood Village, Colorado 80112
(303) 694-1664 or FAX (303) 694-4098
www.pantrypress.com

Please ship _____ copies of *Best of the Historic West.* (for shipments to destinations outside of the United States, please call prior to ordering)

$21.95 per copy	_____
$ 3.50 shipping per copy (USA only)	_____
Colorado residents please add 3.8% sales tax	_____
TOTAL	_____

Make check payable to: **StarsEnd Creations**

Ship To: Name_____

Address _____ __

City_____ State ____ Zip _____

Please allow three weeks for delivery

Pantry Press

3547 E. Arapahoe Road, #J224
Greenwood Village, Colorado 80112
(303) 694-1664 or FAX (303) 694-4098
www.pantrypress.com

Please ship _____ copies of *Seasoned Greetings.* (for shipments to destinations outside of the United States, please call prior to ordering)

$21.95 per copy	_____
$ 3.50 shipping per copy (USA only)	_____
Colorado residents please add 3.8% sales tax	_____
TOTAL	_____

Make check payable to: **StarsEnd Creations**

Ship To: Name_____

Address _____ __

City_____ State ____ Zip _____

Please allow three weeks for delivery

Cooking Tips

Metric Conversions

1 teaspoon = 5 milliliters
1 tablespoon = 15 milliliters
1 cup =≈ $^1/4$ liter
1 pint = .4732 liter
1 quart = .9463 liter
1 gallon = 3.785 liters
1 ounce =≈ 30 grams
1 pound =≈ 454 grams
1 teaspoon =≈ 3 grams
1 centimeter = .394 inch
1 meter = 39.37 inches
1 inch = 2.54 centimeters

Equivalents

8 ounces = 1 cup
2 cups = 1 pint
2 pints = 1 quart
4 quarts = 1 gallon
60 drops = $^1/3$ teaspoon
1 teaspoon = $^1/3$ tablespoon
3 teaspoons = 1 tablespoon
2 tablespoons = 1 fl. ounce
4 tablespoons = $^1/4$ cup
5$^1/3$ tablespoons = $^1/3$ cup
8 tablespoons = $^1/2$ cup
16 tablespoons = 1 cup
$^1/4$ cup = 2 ounces
1 cup = 8 ounces =
16 tablespoons =
48 teaspoons

Temperatures

Water freezes at 32°
At Sea Level:
Water simmers at 115°
Water scalds at 130°
Water boils at 212°
Soft boil at 234-238°
Firm boil at 240-242°
Hard boil at 248-250°
Slow oven 268°
Moderate oven 350°
Deep fat 375-400°
Hot oven 450-500°
Broil 550°
At 5,000 Feet:
Water boils at 203°
At 10,000 Feet:
Water boils at 194°

Low Altitude Adjustments

Since all of the ranches contributing recipes for this cookbook are located at high altitude, the recipes have already been adjusted for this factor. In order to have the dishes turn out the way they were intended, cooks at altitudes below 3,000 feet above sea level should make some adjustments.

When preparing these dishes at a lower altitude, please note that the time to boil foods will be decreased. Also, there will need to be a change in the proportions of ingredients used in leavened foods such as cakes; increasing the amount of leavening and/or sugar, for example. In some cases it will be necessary to adjust the baking temperature as well. Should this become necessary the general rule is to decrease the oven temperature 25 degrees when baking batters and dough. Repeated experimentation is sometimes necessary before the correct procedure is arrived at for low altitude baking.

General guidelines to follow are:

Increase baking powder $^1/8$ to $^1/4$ teaspoon for each teaspoon

Increase sugar 1 to 3 tablespoons for each cup

Decrease liquid 1 to 4 tablespoons for each cup

Glossary

Spices and Herbs

Allspice

Used whole in soups, stews, pot roasts, sauces and marinades, boiled, steamed or poached seafood. Used ground in cakes, cookies, candy, spaghetti and barbecue sauces, sweet potatoes or squash, chili, tomato sauces.

Basil

Used whole or ground with lamb, fish, roasts, stews, ground beef, vegetables, dressing and omelets.

Bay Leaves

Whole leaf is used, but must be removed before serving. Good in vegetable dishes, fish and seafood, stews and pickles.

Caraway

Its spicy smell and aromatic taste goes well with cakes, breads, soups, cheese and sauerkraut.

Chives

An herb with a sweet mild onion flavor that is excellent in salads, fish, soups and potatoes.

Cinnamon

Used whole in pickling and preserving, hot chocolate, mulled wine, stewed fruit and compotes. Ground it can be used in cookies, cakes, French toast, dessert sauces, sweet potatoes and squash, lamb roast, stews, ham glaze, apple sauce and butter, puddings and custard.

Cloves

Used whole as a garnish for ham, fruit peels, onions, glazed pork or beef, beverages, pot roast, marinades and sauces. Ground it goes well in cakes, gingerbread, plum pudding, cookies, breads, fruit salad, chili sauce, green vegetables, meringue, glazes and mincemeat.

Dill

Both seeds and leaves are flavorful when used as either a garnish or cooked in fish, soup, dressings, potatoes and beans.

Fennel

Seeds and leaves are used. Sweet hot flavor that can be used sparingly in pies, baked goods or boiled with fish.

Glossary

Garlic

Used primarily in tomato dishes, soups and sauces, dips, butter, gravy, meat, poultry and fish. Also used in salad dressings and cheese dishes.

Ginger

A pungent root that can be used either fresh, dried or ground. Used in pickling and preserving, cakes, cookies, soups and meat dishes.

Marjoram

Can be used fresh or dried. Flavors fish, poultry, omelets, lamb stew, stuffing and tomato juice.

Mint

Excellent in beverages, fish, cheese, lamb, soup, peas, carrots and fruit desserts.

Nutmeg

Used in sweet foods such as cakes, cookies, pies or pastries. Enhances the flavor of meats, vegetables, poultry, seafood, eggnog, fruit, puddings and soups.

Oregano

Used whole or ground to spice tomato juice, fish, eggs, pizza, omelets, chili, stew, gravy, poultry and vegetables.

Paprika

Used in meat, vegetables and soups. Can be used as a garnish for potatoes, salads or eggs.

Parsley

Best fresh, but can be used dry in fish, omelets, soup, meat, stuffing and mixed greens.

Rosemary

Used to season fish, stuffing, beef, lamb, poultry, onions, eggs and bread.

Saffron

Used as flavoring or to color foods. Used in soup, chicken, rice and fancy breads.

Sage

May be used in tomato juice, fish, fondue, omelets, beef, poultry, stuffing, cheese spreads, cornbread and biscuits.

Glossary

Tarragon

Flavor sauces, salads, meat, poultry, tomatoes and dressings.

Thyme

Used in meat, poultry and fish. Combines well with butter over vegetables or broiled seafood. Good in stuffing for fish and meats, cheese and tomato dishes or clam chowder.

Cooking Terms

Au gratin

Topped with crumbs and/or cheese and browned in the oven or under the broiler.

Au jus

Served in its own juices.

Baste

To moisten foods during cooking with pan drippings or special sauce to add flavor and prevent drying.

Bisque

A thick cream soup.

Blanch

To immerse in rapidly boiling water and allow to cook slightly.

Cream

To soften a fat, especially butter, by beating it at room temperature.

Crimp

To seal the edges of a two-crust pie either by pinching them at intervals with the fingers or by pressing them together with the tines of a fork.

Degrease

Removal of fat from the surface of stews, soups or stock.

Dredge

Lightly coat with flour, cornmeal, crumbs, etc.

Entrée

The main course.

Fold

Incorporating a delicate substance, such as whipped cream or beaten egg whites, into another substance without releasing air bubbles.

Glossary

Glaze

To cover with a glossy coating, such as melted and somewhat diluted jelly for fruit desserts.

Julienne

Cutting vegetables, fruits or cheeses into match-sized slivers.

Marinate

To leave food soaking in a liquid in order to tenderize or add flavor.

Meuniere

Dredged with flour and sautéed in butter.

Mince

Chopping or cutting food into very small pieces.

Parboil

To boil until partially cooked.

Pare

Removal of the outermost skin of a fruit or vegetable.

Poach

Cooking very gently in a liquid that is kept just below the boiling point.

Puree

To mash foods until perfectly smooth by hand, rubbing through a sieve or food mill, or by whirling in a blender or food processor.

Sauté

Cooking or browning food in a small quantity of oil or butter.

Scald

Heating just below the boiling point.

Simmer

Cook in liquid just below the boiling point.

Steep

To let food stand in hot liquid to extract or the enhance flavor.

Toss

Combining ingredients with a lifting motion.

Whip

To beat rapidly to incorporate air and produce expansion.

Notes